THE
COTTAGE GARDEN

THE
COTTAGE GARDEN

CHRISTOPHER LLOYD
& RICHARD BIRD

PHOTOGRAPHY BY
JACQUI HURST

DORLING KINDERSLEY LONDON

A Dorling Kindersley Book

First published in Great Britain in 1990
by Dorling Kindersley Limited,
9 Henrietta Street, London WC2E 8PS

British Library Cataloguing in Publication Data
Lloyd, Christopher 1921–
     The cottage garden.
     1. Country gardens. Cultivation
     I. Title   II. Bird, Richard

ISBN 0–86318–415–4

Editor Susan Thompson   **Art Editor** Gill Della Casa   **Designer** Amanda Lunn
Managing Editor Jane Laing   **Managing Art Editor** Alex Arthur

Typeset by Bookworm Typesetting, Manchester
Reproduced by Columbia in Singapore
Printed and bound by Kyodo-Shing Loong Printing Industries PTE Limited in Singapore

CONTENTS

THE COTTAGE-GARDEN TRADITION 6

COTTAGE-GARDEN PLANTS 16

COTTAGE-GARDEN FEATURES 102

PLANNING THE COTTAGE GARDEN 130

THE WORKING COTTAGE GARDEN 161

THE COTTAGE-GARDEN TRADITION

THE ESSENCE OF A COTTAGE GARDEN as it has come down to us through the ages is a bountiful yet regulated informality. It has evolved through common sense, combines need with enjoyment and is entirely unpretentious.

The layout could be said to be formal, as the front path invariably leads straight from the gate to the door. Vegetables, of course, are planted in neat rows, as are currant and gooseberry bushes, strawberries and raspberry canes. But the flowers are a happy jumble. There are no large groups. A plant is pushed in wherever a large enough gap can be found. Many are there by virtue of having sown themselves.

The cottage walls are plastered with climbers and wall fruits. There are herbs close to the kitchen door. The emphasis, apart from fruit and vegetables, is definitely on flowers rather than foliage. There are none of your grey foliage plants unless they are also herbs like lavender cotton (*Santolina*) or that pungently scented shrub, *Artemisia abrotanum*, whose vernacular names – old man, southernwood, lad's-love – bear witness to its long-standing popularity.

A trim box hedge edging the path is not typical of the cottage garden but closer akin to the more prosperous owner's knot garden of Elizabethan times. The cottager knows nothing of this but might well have a ball- or oval-shaped box bush near the gate or front door. The path might be lined with London pride or thrift, but more generally it is with plants that spill over the path's margin during their summer luxuriance.

A Tidy Mess

Although appearing free and easy, the best kind of cottage garden is actually well organized, otherwise nature would take over, and nature is no gardener (except in the high Alps). But the borders flanking the front path are mixed as are the colours. Bright colours abound but they have not the harshness that has crept into the colouring of modern roses.

Perhaps it is rather a question of which flower wears the colour than of the colour itself. The scarlet *Lychnis chalcedonica*, or Maltese cross, was introduced as long ago as 1593 and fits perfectly in any cottage-garden setting, but translated to a rose – which has been possible only for the past forty years at most – its colour looks absurdly modern, as does the shape of the flower and the habit of the bush.

ATTENDING A SKEP A bee-keeper from yesteryear attends to a skep, the traditional style of beehive. The modern WBC hive is more practical, although less picturesque.

ALWAYS ROOM FOR FLOWERS A rock rose, Cistus sp., and a shrub rose spill out through the wooden fence of this tiny front garden.

Rustic Charm

Materials are indicative, too. Your cottage-garden gate is wooden, not of heavily wrought iron painted in shining black. Neither is the path of concrete, nor even of concrete imitating stone, in rectangles or squares, but of some local material. In my village, where there is much clay and where a brickyard existed when I was young, the path is of bricks, laid on edge for strength. They might form a herringbone design. In chalk country, flint is the natural choice, and near to the sea, it is shingle cobbles. Where the owner is a craftsman with an eye for design, a delightful, patterned mixture of paving materials is used.

Changing Emphasis

An expectation of bees and beehives in the cottage garden is often disappointed today, but was once a natural adjunct as was the home pig and sty, even rarer in these days of affluence and mobile owners. Neither will you see the large mongrel tied by his chain with kennel nearby. The well was also

once a common feature with the simplest of winches to raise the bucket. Perhaps it had a pump, but never an elaborate well-head.

There was always a bench outside the door, and that you would certainly still expect to see. Cottages have small windows and the cottager has always liked to sit inside with the door open, or outside whenever the weather allowed.

Enduring Characteristics

The appeal of the cottage garden is in its friendly intimacy. There are no empty spaces, no lawns, no vistas. Everything is near at hand and the good scents of flowers like roses, honeysuckle, lavender and mignonette are trapped. These advantages have been enjoyed by the well-to-do for many years and thus the cottage-garden tradition is unlikely to die.

Early Days

Living at subsistence level, the peasant cottager of medieval times had little interest in flowers and preferred meat, when he could get it, to vegetables. Medicinal herbs were important but not for their appearance and it seems to me that there is not much point today in growing herbs that are neither beautiful nor useful.

By Elizabethan times there was a bit more money around. Vegetables were being grown, including (rather surprisingly, since it has never really caught on in the British diet) the globe artichoke. This would not be so much by the lowest kind of labourer as by the independent small farmer and his wife. Rhubarb was used but only the root for medicinal purposes.

Among flowers, Thomas Tusser, in the mid-sixteenth century, mentions violets for a number of purposes: for use in cooking (as were primroses and pot marigolds – *Calendula*); for strewing on the floor against noxious smells and to ward off vermin; and for their own sake. The bay laurel, *Laurus nobilis*, was included as well as plants such as sweet williams and hollyhocks, which were grown for pleasure.

Influences from Abroad

The Crown imperial fritillary, so popular with the Dutch flower painters, arrived in England before 1690 and soon filtered through to cottage gardens. Indeed, these gardeners were greatly influenced by Flemish, Walloon and French artisan refugees (weavers in particular). They brought with them a taste for florists' flowers, flowers which were hybridized for improvement in size and form and which were the subjects for competitive exhibition, particularly in the north. They also brought a taste for well-cooked vegetables, which assumed greater importance in the English cottager's diet from then on. The Scots still seem to be content to this day with potatoes and neaps (turnips)! The potato itself, introduced in Elizabethan times, was gradually popularized in Great Britain through the seventeenth century (much more rapidly in Ireland, but there has never been a cottage-garden tradition there).

WATCHING THE PASSERS-BY This cottager takes a rest from her labours to look over her garden fence and watch the passers-by in the world beyond her garden.

A TANGLE OF GREEN AROUND THE COTTAGE DOOR Entering this cottage entails forging your way through the vigorous honesty that forms a screen across the doorway.

A Precarious Existence

Although the chief difference between a cottage garden and an allotment is permanence, the cottager was frequently under threat of expulsion at the whim of his landlord. In the eighteenth century, when the system of enclosures was under way, complete villages were sometimes destroyed, while common land disappeared. The cottager had no redress. However, if the squire was conscientious, the village was rebuilt or the tenant was able to continue in his original cottage for generations.

The Cottager's Lot Improves

The genuine labouring cottager of the nineteenth century was better off, although still badly paid, because there were numerous vocal reformers chipping away at the social conscience of well-to-do landowners. John Claudius Loudon was among the most effective in the gardening world and, with his honesty combined with expertise, he still makes refreshing reading.

Through him and the contributors to his *The Gardener's Magazine*, the cottager was frequently given a considerably larger garden than he had been used to. It was suggested that with 20 rods (600yd^2/480m^2) of land a cottager could feed a family of five if he followed one of Loudon's garden proposals. If the cottage stood near the road, then the small front garden consisted entirely of flowers with the production area behind. If it stood back, then flowers lined the front path, while vegetables and fruit flanked them on either side. The same arrangement holds good today, although pressures on garden size have much increased with our shortages of building land.

The Cottage Gentry

The genuine cottager began to be joined, towards the end of the eighteenth century, by members of the gentry seeking "the good life" – a simpler life nearer to the soil but with money and independence to back them up. Our idea of cottage gardening today owes much to this trend and when we emulate the cottage-garden style (as I do, to an extent in my own garden and its treatment), it is not because of the necessity to grow food, but because we are keen to

SCRAPING POTATOES This old lady scrapes a pail of potatoes on the garden bench outside the kitchen door.

BEAUTIFUL RETREAT It is hard to imagine a more tranquil scene than this garden, which is filled with cottage flowers.

adopt a free-and-easy style and to grow our vegetables on soil laced with dung and garden compost rather than with man-made fertilizers (which also have their place, I would hasten to add). Also it is because we want to foster some of our own wild flowers or derivatives (like coloured primroses and cowslips) not too far removed.

We may not be prepared to keep bees, but we like to see them working on flowers that they like and that we will grow, in part, with the bees in mind. The culinary herbs from our own patch taste better for being freshly gathered or frozen green, rather than used dry from a jar.

Widespread Influences of the Cottage Style

William Robinson (born 1838) was in the Loudon tradition. Even when planting on a large scale, his ideal was of the traditional English cottage garden. So influences from below were percolating upwards instead of the other way about.

It is the influence of the cottage garden, rather than the gardens themselves, which we see mainly today. The two streams of cottage gardening – the authentic and the recreated – continued throughout the nineteenth century and well into the twentieth, when the former began to disappear until there were very

few true examples left. Gardeners since the last war have been increasingly bombarded with advice from the television and the press and have plants of a standard uniformity readily available from their local garden centre. This has all but removed the almost naive and intuitive style of planting that was practised in the past.

The Heyday of Cottage-gardening Style

It was this style that influenced the Victorians – gardeners such as William Robinson and, later, Gertrude Jekyll. They recognized a genuine style from which they were able to extract some essential elements – informality, for example – which they then applied to their own designs. The influence of these two gardeners can still be felt, in particular in

PASTEL SHADES (left) Dusky purple, pink and white create pleasing, subtle tones in this wilderness of a garden.

BENEFITS OF A DITCH This couple cheerfully clear the peripheral ditch, which keeps the cottage free from the water that drains off surrounding fields.

the garden created by Vita Sackville-West and her husband at Sissinghurst and the earlier garden at Hidcote, laid out by Lawrence Johnston. Although they are patently on a larger scale than that of a true cottage garden, these planting schemes and the intimate atmosphere they create have a strong feel of the authentic about them.

To a large extent it is gardens such as these and the chocolate-box images conjured up by the romantic Victorian artists, such as Myles Birket Foster and Helen Allingham, rather than the sight of real cottage gardens that inspire so many people today to try to recreate this type of garden.

Waning Popularity

The ancestors of these cottage gardens still exist – the allotment in particular still echoes certain elements – but generally the type of garden that inspired Gertrude Jekyll is now difficult to find. Vegetables are still grown but nowhere near as widely as even thirty or so years ago. The herbaceous plants and self-seeding annuals have been replaced by lawns and patios and the flower beds themselves converted into low-maintenance groupings of shrubs and bedding plants, tidiness being the watch-word. One must not give the impression that there are no exciting gardens around – there are many – but nearly all these have a conscious guiding hand behind them.

Unfortunately, it is impossible to turn back the clock, and in the main we are all too sophisticated, in a gardening way, to create a genuine cottage garden, but we can *re*create one based on our and other people's idea of the past. There is nothing wrong with this: the style is as valid now, at the end of the twentieth century, as it was at the time of William Robinson and Gertrude Jekyll.

Growing for Competition

Cottage gardens have often been an unconscious display of the gardener's ability; a more conscious display was, and still is, made at the village show. This is one aspect that has been kept alive. A surprising number of small villages still have their annual competition: for some, entry is deadly serious, for others just fun. The classes have changed little down the years and many shows still have a class for the best "cottage garden", often won these days by council-house gardens, which, in many respects, are the ones that are keeping alive some of the cottage-garden tradition.

Many of these shows owe their origin to the florist feasts, which go back to the seventeenth century. Florists, until the change in meaning of the word towards the end of the nineteenth century, were gardeners whose interest in plants was for their decorative, rather than culinary or medicative, value. Originally they were mainly concerned with a small group of plants, which included anemones, pinks and tulips, but gradually these increased in numbers. They formed specialist societies and held competitions, often held at public houses, which often included junketing and other jollifications, hence "florist feasts". Many of their early plants originated as selections from the wild but as more plants came in from abroad they were able to increase their range.

A Taste for Roses (right) The owner of this garden indulges her preference for roses, the queen of cottage flowers, planting them up throughout this front garden.

Pretty as a Picture This young girl poses by the cottage gate in her Sunday best, surrounded by fragrant lilies and climbing roses.

Traditional Cottage Plants & Planting

New plant introductions from abroad were at their peak in the nineteenth century and many of these, inevitably, found their way into and were assimilated by cottage gardens. I don't think we need ever feel too hide-bound in our notions of what a cottage gardener should grow. It was subject to outside influences in the past and there is no need to fix it for eternity. But there are some kinds of plant about which one may say that they seem right in the cottage garden whereas others, highly developed by the hybridizers, look completely out of place.

Ironically these have frequently been bred as dwarfs for the very reason that space is nowadays so limited, and this is obviously relevant to the cottage as well as to the town and suburban garden. Yet a dwarfed plant with large flowers, such as one of the Inca marigolds, has lost its freedom and its natural style of growth and this is essential to cottage flowers. If a cottage garden can accommodate a 7ft (210cm) hollyhock, as is patently the case, it can accommodate any size of annual or perennial, but fewer plants of each.

No groups are found in the cottage garden unless they are formed by purely natural means. For example, it could be that a plant is a prolific self-seeder or spreads rapidly by runners, but even then it is likely to be discouraged from increasing too much because of the lack of space. Formality is also very rare. There might be a row of London pride or double daisies or of violas along the front path on either side, but nothing more repetitive than that until you reach the well-ordered rows of vegetables and soft fruit.

A few fruit trees would be expected, where space allowed, and perhaps an unproductive but popular tree like the rowan, in Scotland, to ward off evil spirits, or the laburnum, which again has a long tradition in Scotland.

The Scottish Influence

The cottage garden is recognizable right up the centre and east of Scotland to Orkney. That a leek should be called Musselburgh or a strain of stocks, East Lothian, is no accident. But in the West Highlands the crofts rarely have gardens. Their long history of poverty, insecurity and clearances to make way for sheep, did not allow for gardening and now, even in better times, the shambles continues, with old cars and refrigerators dumped just outside the croft.

ONE

COTTAGE-GARDEN PLANTS

The cottager has always been partial to bright, exuberant flowers and the first thing you notice about a cottage garden is the abundance and variety of its plants. Grown in a jumble in the borders, you can scarcely see bare earth between the flowers.

This chapter features all the popular, traditional cottage-garden plants. Photographed both in groups in the cottage garden and as individual portraits, they are grouped under the following headings: plants for winter, fragrant plants, double-blooming plants, wild plants, annuals and biennials, plants for bees and butterflies, perennials, traditional shrubs, herbs, fruit and vegetables. Many of the plants are also grouped according to flowering season to help you decide which to choose for your garden.

The authors provide plenty of information on growing and caring for the plants featured in this chapter, which enables you to stock your cottage garden with only those plants truly suited to it.

FLOWERING PLANTS

To many people, the expression "cottage garden" evokes a cheerful jumble of brightly coloured, flowering plants with not a speck of soil showing between them. In fact, plants that are grown purely for their flowers are relative newcomers to the cottage garden, which was originally filled with productive plants, such as herbs and vegetables.

Many herbs have attractive flowers and it was probably these that encouraged the cottager to grow prettier, though less useful, plants. Even then, his choice of flowers was dictated not so much by fashion as by practical considerations, such as availability. A shortage of money led the cottager to take plants from the wild or to choose cultivated plants that were easy to propagate. The more unusual plants he included came from the large gardens of the gentry. The gardener employed there would take home part

of a plant, such as a division, or a couple of bulbs while thinning a clump. Then, if the plant grew well, the next season he would give a piece to his neighbour who in turn would give to his neighbour until the plant was resident in all the local gardens. So it might be said that cottage-garden flowers today are hardy, pretty and increase easily.

The flowers in a cottage garden had to be tough enough to look after themselves. Most cottagers were too busy to spend time on the flowers. They worked long hours in the fields and what free time they had was devoted to tending edible plants – vegetables and herbs – so often vital to their livelihood. Flowers came second. And as no one could give their attention to weak-growing species or plants prone to disease, most of the old-fashioned cottage-garden favourites were strong growing – a reason why so many have survived, even in neglected gardens – to be here for us to enjoy today.

The cottage gardener had little interest in complicated propagation techniques either. It is the herbaceous plants, easily divided by crudely chopping them in pieces with a spade and replanting them, that have come down to us, rather than those plants dependent on propagation by cuttings.

In many ways, the flower garden was labour-saving. The plants grew close enough to support one another and also to supress weeds. And annuals and biennials, such as poppies and foxgloves, tended to self-sow, meaning that they usually demanded only a little attention.

Such low-maintenance techniques – sowing plants closely together and choosing the self-seeding species – can be used in the cottage garden today. Remember, though, that it is essential that the soil is always well prepared before planting begins.

OBSCURED PATH This garden path is virtually obscured by the exuberant plants that edge it.

WINDOW DRESSING A simple window is set off to perfection by a bank of vivid cottage flowers and a lace curtain.

WINTER PLANTS

WITH THEIR ASSURANCE that life is still pulsing in the natural world, winter flowers have an appeal close to every gardener's heart. All hellebores, including the Christmas rose, *Helleborus niger*, are suited to cottage gardens, but the native *Helleborus fastidious* strikes me as the most beautiful of all. It is semi-shrubby, the leaves are very dark and divided into fingers about an arc, and are arranged in a loose rosette on each evergreen shoot. The compound inflorescence of the bell flower is pale green and is at its peak from

JOY OF WINTER The common snowdrop, Galanthus nivalis, is one of the great joys of winter. Once established, it multiplies quickly and should be split every few years. As well as single forms there are double varieties, as seen here.

mid-winter to early spring. A fat clump of the white blossoms of Christmas roses, in a moist and shady spot, often against the wall of the cottage, has widespread appeal. But these plants can be temperamental and can also suffer from a nasty botrytis disease.

A hellebore that my mother acquired from a fellow villager was known for long, but alas incorrectly, as *H. atrorubens*. In his monograph on this genus, Brian Mathew proposes the name *H. orientalis* var. *abchasicus* 'Early Purple'. This plant I recommend. It has deep (not deepest) rosy-purple flowers and is always in bloom in my Sussex garden by Christmas, under a totally sunless wall.

Hybrids of the Lenten rose, *H. orientalis*, are all suitable for cottage gardens. Another hellebore that we received from this same village friend has green flowers with heavy purple spotting and speckling towards the base and in the centre of each sepal.

Winter Irises

If hellebores enjoy a shady aspect, the Algerian iris loves to bask against a sunny wall, where it is happy to remain undisturbed for year upon year. The more it is baked (but not entirely starved of water) the better it will flower. The Algerian iris is often known as *Iris stylosa* but should correctly be called *I. unguicularis*, though the clumsy epithet has rarely stuck. There is no greater pleasure than picking its demurely inconspicuous buds to bring indoors and then watch unfurl. Sometimes within minutes, you will see a delightful, silken mauve bloom, too fragile, you would have thought, to flower in winter. A good strain of *I. stylosa* should flower in every mild spell from late autumn to mid-spring. The earliest flowering cultivar that I have come across is the scented *I.s.* 'Walter Butt' with its rather washed-out colouring. *I.s.* 'Mary Barnard' has rich purple blooms, coming into their own in mid-winter.

The other winter iris that I would recommend is *I. histrioides* 'Major', with its deep blue petals (the colour varies markedly), each with a yellow flash. This is a bulbous iris and, as it grows only 2½-4in (6-10cm) tall, it deserves a special position – a trough, sink or rock ledge, for example – so as not to be lost among the other plants.

Winter Shrubs

As mentioned earlier, there is little room for shrubs, and least of all for those that flower in winter but look dull in summer. An exception can be made for the

Chinese witch hazel, *Hamamelis mollis*, because its growth is slow and its size can be controlled by picking twigs or branches for use indoors, where the scent from their winter flowers is best appreciated. Its clusters of ribbon petals are, typically, a warm shade of yellow but, given the space for just the one plant, I prefer the paler yellow *H.m.* 'Pallida', which is a showier plant with longer ribbons.

With this you might care to plant (on acid soil, which *Hamamelis* also prefers) one of the early-flowering, azalea-like rhododendrons, *Rhododendron dauricum* or *R. mucronulatum*, with their rich mauve or purple flowers.

Heathers & Mahonia

Somewhere within the cottage garden there must be a patch of winter-flowering heathers, such as the carmine or white varieties of *Erica carnea*. I like to see these combined with the bright green foliage of a hebe, such as the whipcord *Hebe armstrongii*, or the bush ivy, *Hedera helix* 'Conglomerata', whose densely clothed shoots are held like tapered candles.

It would be difficult to resist a mahonia in a winter cottage garden, and the choice almost inevitably falls on *Mahonia japonica*, whose clustered strands of pale yellow flowers open from mid-autumn to mid-spring and are strongly scented on the air. *M. japonica* tolerates a shady position and its natural tendency to make a large bush can be controlled by pruning it heavily immediately after flowering.

Jasmine & Clematis

Such pruning should also be routine for the winter jasmine, *Jasminum nudiflorum*, whether it is grown against a wall (even one with a shady aspect) or free-standing, perhaps forming a bracket over a ledge. The flowers open from autumn to late winter.

Clematis cirrhosa was introduced from the Mediterranean some 50 years earlier. It is evergreen, with pretty foliage often bronzed in winter. If given a rather hot position, it is likely to carry an abundance of pale green, bell flowers, often speckled red within (and lemon-scented if you bring a sprig indoors). It opens all through the winter.

Forsythia

Few cottage gardens are without forsythia and the traditional species for this purpose is *Forsythia suspensa*. This would be my recommendation, too, since it has a natural grace lost by the later cultivars.

LONG-LASTING BLOOMS For flowers that last for a long period in the winter, choose the Lenten rose, Helleborus orientalis. *Its colour varies from white to deep purple and it is often spotted.*

Its growth, however, is somewhat lax but can be controlled by pruning as soon as it has flowered. Although it is a bit of a cheat to include forsythia as a winter-flowering shrub, it does force readily indoors if cut in mid- to late winter. The earliest naturally flowering species is *F. ovata* and it is a good choice, being of a less assertive yellow than most.

Bulbs

Winter aconites, *Eranthis hyemalis*, can do marvellously well in cottage gardens, spreading without interference by self-sowing. Winter-flowering crocuses planted informally, are also suitable. Good choices are *Crocus sieberi* (pale mauve), *C. fulvus* (rich orange) and, above all, *C. chrysanthus*, which comes in many different shades. *C.* 'Snow Bunting' (white), one of the earliest, smells like honey.

Before moving on to spring flowers I must mention the winter heliotrope, *Petasites fragrans*. It spreads ferociously, and is suited to the bank just outside the garden. The clusters of pale mauve flowers open in early to mid-winter and their sweet scent is no less welcome at that season for being more than a little sickly.

Winter Flowers

We are especially grateful for any flowers in the garden that brighten up the long, grey months of winter.

❖ *WEEPING FORSYTHIA* (Forsythia suspensa) *This graceful, deciduous shrub has slender shoots and narrow, trumpet-shaped, yellow flowers. Prefers full sun and well-drained soil.*

❖ *CHRISTMAS ROSE* (Helleborus niger) *A small evergreen perennial, noted for its lovely cup-shaped white flowers and golden stamens. Prefers partial shade and well-drained soil.*

❖ *CROCUS* (Crocus sieberi 'Bowles White') *The funnel-shaped white flowers of this variety have large yellow centres and exude a delicious perfume. Prefers full sun and well-drained soil.*

❖ *VIBURNUM* (Viburnum tinus) *Numerous, flat heads of tiny pink buds, which open into small, white blooms, clothe this bushy, dense, evergreen shrub. Prefers full sun and well-drained soil.*

❖ *SNOWDROP* (Galanthus elwesii) *This favourite is easy to identify as each inner petal of the pendant white flowers bears green marks at the apex and base. Prefers partial shade and moist soil.*

❖ *WINTER ACONITE* (Eranthis hyemalis) *Cheerful, cup-shaped yellow flowers with leaf-like bracts brighten this clump-forming plant. Prefers partial shade and moist soil.*

DOUBLE FLOWERS

DOUBLE FLOWERS HAVE ALWAYS been particular favourites with the cottager. Not for him the type of sophistication which declares that the simple, single, untrammelled flower, as Dame Nature intended it, is the only kind and that doubles are a travesty. For him the more petals there are, the more flower. Besides, the formality and precision of a double flower is part of its appeal.

As a child I was always fascinated by the double celandines – gleaming yellow becoming green at the centre – on a grassy bank just below the Jones's weather-boarded cottage on our hill. They are still there and nothing will destroy them until that roadside bank is so gentrified that it is dug up and planted with low-maintenance ground cover (dwarf conifers and heathers, most likely).

The wood anemone is so widespread that the many varieties developed from it come as no surprise. I am particularly fond of the late spring-flowering 'Vestal', which is pure white with seven guard petals framing a tight button centre. On its own this button is not unlike the neat, formal flowers of *Ranunculus aconitifolius* 'Flore Pleno', called fair maids of Kent and also fair maids of France. Despite its name, this freely branching, 1½ft- (45cm-) tall plant grows best in particularly cool conditions. In Orkney it is one of the commonest of all garden plants.

Buttercups & Daisies

Most of the buttercups have double flower forms. The largest of them, *Ranunculus speciosus* 'Plenus', is glamorous and has flowers with quite large, green-centred rosettes. I think my favourite is the double form of the field buttercup, *R. acris*, which is 2ft (60cm) tall, well branched, with lots of smallish yellow buttons. The creeping buttercup, *R. repens*, also has a beguiling double form but beware! It sends out runners and roots as it travels.

From buttercups it is natural to turn to daisies. Selected forms of *Bellis perennis*, the daisies that grow in our lawns, were cultivated by cottagers. Where there are no lawns, daisies line the path. Double red-quilled daisies are an old form and so is the amusing kind called hen-and-chickens, in which the central flower is surrounded by a ring of pups – or chicks.

Marigolds are in the daisy family. It is the pot marigold, *Calendula officinalis*, that tunes in with old cottage gardens. It was introduced into Britain from southern Europe in 1573 and was quickly adopted by the herbalists. Everyone prefers the double form and it usually starts that way but is an inveterate self-seeder and soon reverts to a single type. It is attractive to grow though, and its orange petals are one of the prettiest garnishings for salads. So, too, are those of the double, vivid orange nasturtium, *Tropaeolum majus* 'Hermine Gnashof', but it is tender and does not set seed. The cuttings root easily, though, and can be overwintered on a windowsill.

Foreign & Home-grown Doubles

Of peonies, the double kinds (called peeny roses in Scotland) are great cottage favourites, especially the deep crimson-red *Paeonia officinalis* 'Rubra Plena', which flowers in late spring and has a rather

A SPLASH IN SPRING Double peony flowers make a vivid splash of colour in the spring, contrasting well with the strong foliage. They like a place in the sun.

rank smell. There are also double pink and double white forms of this species, which came from southern Europe in the mid-sixteenth century. *P. lactiflora*, from the Far East, did not arrive until the late eighteenth century, but it is a good cottage-garden flower, less frequently diseased in these circumstances and happy to be left undisturbed for some thirty years. The flowers have a fresh rose scent with a slight sharpness added. Doubles have always been the favourites, although they are heavy headed and borne to the ground when filled with rainwater.

Double roses must be mentioned here as no cottage garden is complete without at least one of the old-fashioned favourites. For strong colour, *Rosa* 'Mme Isaac Pereire' is a good choice. It is a Bourbon rose with fragrant, fully double, magenta flowers. More delicately *R.* 'Félicité Perpétue' has clusters of blush pink to white flowers and *R.* 'Blush Noisette' has dainty, fragrant, pink blooms.

WALL OF COLOUR Clothed in red climbing roses, this wall is further decorated with white and red hollyhocks, evening primroses, and a tangle of sweet peas.

Periwinkles, *Vinca minor*, have double blue and double purple variants. I have never met anyone who has seen a double white form, although there have been rumours of its existence. The charming double meadow cranesbill, *Geranium pratense*, is widely available in both blue and white.

Double white arabis is an old favourite as is the double-coloured form of the closely related aubrieta. Dropwort, *Filipendula hexapetala*, grows wild in its single-flowered form on the dry chalk downs but the double is the one that cottagers have cultivated. Sprays of white flowers appear 2ft (60cm) above deep green, ferny leaves. I think it is best grown in the cracks of paving, where its height is reduced, preventing it from falling on its face.

Although apt to be weak stemmed, double oriental poppies, *Papaver orientale*, are a feature of many Scottish cottage gardens, often escaping into roadside verges where, like lupins, they are perfectly happy to cope with rough grass.

Double-flowered soapwort, alias bouncing Bet, *Saponaria officinalis*, is certainly a traditional cottage-garden flower, although I hesitate to recommend a plant whose rootstock runs so aggressively. The flowers may be white, deep or (usually) pale pink.

There is nothing new-fangled about double forms of hollyhock, *Alcea rosea*, and the dark, maroon-coloured forms have long been greatly esteemed. Perhaps they have been too greatly esteemed, to the extent that the specialist's desire is to achieve a truly black flower. Hollyhocks stationed by a cottage entrance look like sentries.

Double primroses, growing in fat clumps in a damp spot in the shade of a cottage or beneath a spreading apple tree, are wholly authentic and a great delight if you can make a success of them. In modern

COUNTRY FAVOURITE Both inside and outside the garden, primroses (Primula vulgaris) have long been a favourite of country people. There are many good garden forms; they come in single and double forms and vary in colour. Some primroses also have a spicy scent.

times, various diseases have tended to devastate stocks of old varieties and one also wonders whether house sparrows were quite so destructive of their flowers in earlier times. But there are as many double-primrose enthusiasts today as ever.

The perennial, peach-leaved bellflower, *Campanula persicifolia*, has been cultivated since the sixteenth century and has many varieties, both blue and white. It likes a stiffish soil and in this it will self-sow generously, perhaps appearing from the middle of a peony crown or from underneath the skirts of a box bush. The double form may either be fully double or, more elegantly, consist of just two rows of petals. Our native, nettle-leaved bellflower, *C. trachelium*, has a pretty though weak-stemmed, double lavender variety called 'Bernice'. Canterbury bells, *C. medium*, are less popular in a double form than the cup-and-saucer, or calycanthema, semi-double form, wherein the saucer is a coloured calyx framing the bell.

Snowdrops & Daffodils

Few experts believe that the snowdrop, *Galanthus nivalis*, is a genuine native, but its cultivation goes back far enough for it to have filled acres of woodland in the course of time. The double snowdrop has been scarcely less successful and even though it does not set seed it seems able to spread itself around. Although its flowers are not very regular or formalized they have great charm, especially when you look down on them. This is a flower that can be fitted into the smallest cottage garden because it will occupy patches that are bare in winter but that become crowded by deciduous shrubs and plants in summer when the snowdrop is dormant.

I don't even know the proper name (if it has one) of the deep-yellow double daffodil, bulbs of which were given to me by a nearby cottager when I was a small child. It looks like a polyploid selection of our native Lent lily, *Narcissus pseudonarcissus*, and, like that, is one of the earliest in flower. Another cottage-garden double is called eggs and bacon. Only the centre, within the cup, is doubled and it is egg-yolk yellow. One should guard against using the thick-stemmed, broad-leaved, large-flowered daffodils and narcissi that have been developed in recent years. Their muscularity and scale is inappropriate in a cottage garden, or on its roadside boundary. Their decaying foliage is obtrusive for many weeks, looking even worse (besides harming the bulbs) when tied into knots.

Cottage Favourites

When introducing plants from the wild into the garden, the cottager has always kept an eye out for the curious and interesting. Double flowers were a natural choice, for they have a voluptuous delicacy that has long endeared them to the cottage gardener. Today these flowers are as popular as ever.

SEMI-DOUBLE WHITE BELLFLOWER (Campanula persicifolia *'Boule de Neige'*) The popular, peach-leaved bellflower comes in an attractive white double form.

DOUBLE CAMPION (Silene dioica *'Rosea Plena'*) This frothy double version of a common hedgerow plant is short-lived, and so needs replacing every few years by dividing the plant.

DOUBLE BUTTERCUP (Ranunculus repens *'Flore Pleno'*) This is an attractive double form of the common but winsome weed.

CINQUEFOIL (Potentilla *'Glory of Nancy'*) This double, herbaceous pontentilla blooms orange and scarlet throughout the summer, adding a strong splash of colour to the border. The colour range is wide, including white, yellow, pink, orange and red.

DOUBLE ROSES (Rosa) Considered by many people to be the most typical of cottage-garden flowers, both shrub and climbing roses produce double forms, many of which are heavily perfumed.

DOUBLE MEADOW
CRANESBILL (Geranium
pratense 'Plenum Album')
The double white form of this
common wild flower may have
been introduced into the cottage
garden from the hedgerow,
where you can easily
obtain the plant.

DOUBLE MEADOW
CRANESBILL (Geranium
pratense 'Plenum
caeruleum') The lilac
blue form of cranesbill
has a wonderfully old-
fashioned look.

YARROW (Achillea ptarmica
'The Pearl') Double forms of this
old cottage flower have been known
since the sixteenth century. It
forms a large clump quickly
and can become a bit
invasive, but it is good
for cutting.

BOUNCING BET
(Saponaria officinalis 'Rosa
Plena') The leaves of this plant,
also known as soapwort, produce
lather that was used for washing
delicate fabrics in the past.

FRAGRANT PLANTS

THERE IS A GOOD DEAL of overlap between double and fragrant flowers. Fragrance has always been highly esteemed, if for no better reason than that it wards off or masks more noisome odours. Our enclosed sewage systems and the habit of frequently bathing and changing our clothes are of recent origin. In the past, nasty smells and the need to disguise them were an accepted fact of life. If flowers could be both fragrant and double, so much the better.

None of these roses blooms for more than a month but then neither do most shrubs. In Scottish cottage gardens you will inevitably meet a plump, twiggy bush or even a hedge, of the double pink, cream, pale yellow or white flowered variety of the Scots or burnet rose. This is *R. pimpinellifolia* (*R. spinosissima*), a native usually found near the sea, up to 3 or 4ft (90 or 120cm) tall, deliciously scented and early flowering. It sports readily from the single cream flower of the wild species and is unquestionably given to suckering. There are also repeat-flowering roses that will bloom for more than a month. Two of the best scented are 'Zéphirine Drouhin' and 'Mme Isaac Pereire' – both Bourbons.

Roses

Favourite cottage-garden roses have always been of the double or cabbage type, although they were not popular in Elizabethan and early seventeenth-century times. The red rose, *Rosa gallica* (*R. rubra*), is still very much with us, especially in its pink-and-red-striped sport 'Rosa Mundi' (*R.g.* 'Versicolor'). And there is the white rose of York, *R.* x *alba*, well known as 'Maiden's Blush'. If you acquire grafted plants of these roses they will sucker from the dog rose stock, and this is insufferable. If on their own roots, they will also sucker incontinently ('Rosa Mundi' often reverting to the plain crimson *R. gallica*). We can do better with less land-hungry varieties and ones that have their own roots: for example, the great double white or Jacobite rose, *R.* x *alba* 'Maxima', which can be grown either as a large, freestanding shrub or against a wall, even one with a shady aspect. 'Celestial' is another wonderful Alba rose, soft pink and exquisite as the bud unfurls. One of the greatest merits of these Alba roses is their handsome glaucous foliage and freedom from disease – no black spot, mildew, or rust.

Of the Gallica types you might choose *Rosa* 'Cristata', the 'Crested Moss' rose – double pink flowers with mossy, spicily scented calyces. The habit is lanky but no one will notice in a cottage-garden border with blue *Campanula persicifolia* coming up through the middle of it and some delphiniums (perhaps the double blue 'Alice Artindale') growing behind. Although a modern rose, 'Constance Spry' has the appearance of a Gallica-style cabbage and is appropriate to the cottage garden, with its full pink blossoms and extraordinary scent, described by Graham Thomas as that of myrrh.

Some roses are particularly good at scenting the air. The Hybrid Musks 'Penelope', 'Felicia' and 'Cornelia' come to mind, as does the miniature Hybrid Tea-style 'Perle d'Or', which forms a sizeable bush.

Gillyflowers

The name gillyflower has been attached to several kinds of flower, all fragrant and often double. The common wallflower, *Cheiranthus cheiri*, was the winter gillyflower. On light soil it is likely to be long-lived and is particularly at home in the rotten mortar of an old wall. The double seed strains are now rarely offered and only the yellow 'Harpur Crewe' is worth growing as it survives virus diseases well.

The stock gillyflower is *Matthiola incana, M. sinuata* and hybrids between them. The word stock means stick or stem, and the plant was so named because old stock plants develop woody stems, which last for years. Only double stocks are welcome in the cottage garden, the singles being used merely for the seed that they produce.

Sweet rocket or dame's violet, *Hesperis matronalis*, deliciously perfumed at night, was also known as Queen's gillyflower. The double form was greatly prized and is still around in cottage gardens today, much less ravaged by virus disease than it used to be. The mauve-and-white singles are mainly cottage flowers of Scotland.

LATE-SUMMER PERFUME Border phloxes, Phlox paniculata, *provide colour and perfume during the late summer. Some varieties have more scent than others, so choose carefully. Behind them grow Shasta daisies.*

PERFUMED DAMASK ROSES Old-fashioned shrub roses are welcome for their heavy, sweet scent as well as the soft colours they contribute to the garden. Giant onion heads jostle beside these Damask roses.

The gillyflower, unqualified, referred to the clove carnation, *Dianthus caryophyllus* (the clove itself was at one time *Caryophyllus aromatica*). Especially in its double red forms, the clove carnation has a rich clove scent that, in chemical analysis, is very close to the clove's own aroma.

Pinks & Sweet Williams

Pinks arise from other species of *Dianthus* and are old favourites. Laced pinks were developed by the artisans of Paisley in the late eighteenth century. The margins of each petal are patterned in a darker colour. 'Dad's Favourite' is still popular. The double white 'Mrs Sinkins' (introduced in 1868) certainly has a wonderful scent but it is an ugly flower, with its calyx invariably split. We can do better than 'Mrs Sinkins' and grow 'White Ladies', which makes a good substitute. 'Inchmery' is a lovely plant, dating from the eighteenth century: soft pink and loosely double, its flowers are very sweet.

Mule pinks date back to the early eighteenth century and are crosses between sweet williams and carnations. Being sterile, they flower almost con-tinuously (even in winter) but, as with many pinks, the plants become woody within a couple of seasons and should be renewed from cuttings.

Sweet williams themselves have a long history. Popped in among other plants, they epitomize a cottage border, the doubles no less than the singles. Sometimes a plant will last for several years but it is usually better replaced with an annual after flowering.

Lilies-of-the-Valley

Lilies-of-the-valley have the cottage-garden temperament – a preference for being left alone. Woodland plants by nature, they are usually sited against a shady wall where they will continue to grow thicker and thicker, not always flowering freely. They are travellers and often seem to prefer the spot where you didn't really want them. In my experience they flower more freely in the sun but grow less luxuriantly. Above all they love the company of other plants.

GUARANTEED FAVOURITE Lily-of-the-valley, Convallaria majalis, *is always a popular choice.*

DAINTY AND DRAMATIC These two pinks highlight the variety within the genus Dianthus. *A frilled double pink grows next to a single with a contrasting centre.*

HAPPY PARTNERSHIP The fragrant blossoms of a pink are offset by the white flowers of Cerastium tomentosum.

Spring Bulbs

The early bulbs are one of the joys of spring. They are the first sign that the garden is awakening after winter.

❖ *GRAPE HYACINTH* (Muscari neglectum) *Numerous, deep blue or blackish blue flowers clothe each spike of this quickly spreading bulb. Prefers full sun and well-drained soil.*

❖ *NARCISSUS* (Narcissus 'Merlin') *Broad white petals surround a dainty, rich gold cup with a lightly ruffled orange-red rim on this variety of narcissus. Prefers full sun and well-drained soil.*

❖ *TULIP* (Tulipa 'Balalaika') *Tulips come in a range of colours and forms. This has a bright red, single flower with yellow base and black stamen. Prefers full sun and well-drained soil.*

❖ *MEADOW SNOWFLAKE* (Leucojum adestivum) *These pendant white flowers are bigger and bloom slightly later than the more familiar snowdrops. Prefers partial shade and moist soil.*

❖ *CROWN IMPERIAL* (Fritillaria imperialis) *Each majestic stalk carries five bell-shaped, orange flowers crowned by small, leaf-like bracts. Prefers full sun and well-drained soil.*

❖ *SPANISH BLUEBELL* (Hyacinthoides hispanica) *Pendant, bell-shaped blue, white or pink flowers loosely adorn each flower spike. Prefers partial shade and moist soil.*

Most of all they love the company of Solomon's seal, *Polygonatum*. Although without scent, this must be mentioned here. *P. x hybridum* is a plant of great style with its arching habit, 2–3ft (60–90cm) tall, its double row of spreading leaves and the greenish bell flowers that hang beneath them in late spring when the lilies-of-the-valley are also blooming.

Madonna Lilies

Turning to real lilies, the Madonna lily, *Lilium candidum*, is the epitome of cottage-garden success, with a flower that more sophisticated gardeners find difficult to grow. This has one of the sweetest scents of all. Flowering in mid-summer, it makes a dense, shortish spike of open white funnels with yellow anthers. A group of thriving lilies should be left alone – in a cottage garden they will be. But if one needs replanting, this should be done on a fresh site, as lilies, like roses, suffer from the mysterious replant disease. The two serious diseases of *L. candidum* are botrytis (the grey-mould fungus that defoliates the stem before flowering has started) and virus. You must have healthy stock at the outset. There is no better way to ensure this than by begging a bulb or two from the owner of a healthy colony. Take them while in flower or soon after (new growth starts in late summer), and plant so that the top of the bulb is only just below the soil surface.

It is worth mentioning that cultivating broken tulips in the same garden as Madonna lilies is a hazard. The tulips' beautiful, streaky flowers, in which the underlying white or yellow pigment shows side by side with the brighter colours, are infected with (but tolerant of) the same viruses that afflict lilies, and the Madonnas are particularly sensitive.

Cottage-garden flowers are generally healthy because they are so varied; there is seldom more than one kind of plant. It is when the enthusiast is tempted to specialize by growing many varieties of one kind of flower – be it roses, lilies, clematis or gladioli – that the pests and diseases move in. They then increase quickly to epidemic strength because of an abundance of their host plants.

Turk's Cap & Crown Imperial Lilies

There are other lilies of cottage-garden status. The purple turk's cap, *L. martagon*, and another turk's cap, *L. pyrenaicum*, are European lilies and were with us by Elizabethan times. Both exude a rank odour, but you can accustom yourself to it. *L. martagon* will spread freely by self-sowing. It is a little murky in colour itself; the prettiest variety is the albino, 'Album', which is a pure white with yellow stamens. *L. pyrenaicum* has greenish-yellow, speckled flowers and grassy foliage. It multiplies into dense colonies in Scotland and the north of England.

The Crown imperial lily was another early introduction, and its wonderful stateliness and symmetry have long made it a favourite in paintings and embroideries. It is an obliging plant if it likes you but in many gardens it produces a high proportion of blind shoots. The Crown imperial lily is not, in fact, a true lily but a *Fritillaria* – *F. imperialis*. It has a rank odour, combining fox with onion scent. The bell flowers, at 3 to 4ft (90–120cm), are brownish-orange or yellow and form a circlet above which grows a tuft of leaf-like bracts. If you lift these and look into a bell, the teardrop nectaries sparkle at you, one at the base of each petal. Flowering is in mid-spring, which is early for so flamboyant a plant. The bulbs, if they need disturbing, should be moved soon after flowering and planted just below the soil surface.

SCENTED LILIES One of the most highly scented lilies, the flowers of the golden-rayed lily, Lilium auratum, *appear in late summer. Protect them from full sun.*

Cottage Favourites

*Flowers that give pleasure to the nose and the eye
are welcome in a cottage garden. Relaxing in such a garden on a warm
summer's evening when the air is heavy with perfume is one of life's
greatest pleasures. Fortunately fragrant plants are not difficult to
acquire, and it is well within the cottager's means to add a few to the
borders. Plants bedded near a window or door will
perfume the inside of the house as well.*

BORDER PHLOX (Phlox
paniculata) *An old favourite,
the perfumed flowers of this
phlox make a valuable
contribution to the border in
late summer. There are
many cultivars
from which to
choose.*

JASMINE (Jasminum officinale)
*A vigorous climbing shrub, the
white flowers of which produce
its characteristic scent on
warm summer evenings.
Jasmine is particularly good
for planting near a window
or in an area for sitting out.*

SWEET PEA (Lathyrus
odoratus *'Painted Lady')
Grown in the flower borders,
in separate rows or possibly
in the vegetable garden,
sweet peas have long been
associated with the cottage
garden. Be sure to choose
an old-fashioned variety
for good scent.*

REGAL LILY (Lilium
regale) *Pink in bud,
opening to a
glistening white
with a touch of pink
on the outside and
extremely fragrant, this is
one of the trumpet lilies most
suited to the cottage garden.*

PINK (Dianthus squarrosus)
Pinks have a history as long as
the cottage garden and no
garden is complete without one.
This species has delicate, deeply
frilled petals and a very strong
clove scent. Choose your
variety carefully as not all
modern cultivars
are perfumed.

LAVENDER (Lavandula
angustifolia) *Another
traditional favourite in
the cottage garden,
lavender flowers retain
their scent when dried and
can be used in the house in
pot-pourri or in sachets for
perfuming linen.*

*LATE DUTCH
HONEYSUCKLE*
(Lonicera periclymenum
'Serotina') *The heady
perfume of honeysuckle is
an important
constituent of any
cottage garden.*

LAVENDER COTTON
(Santolina chamaecyparissus)
*The silver, outer leaves of this
plant are highly
aromatic and
can be dried for winter
use. The buttonlike,
yellow flowers
appear in mid-
summer.*

Jasmine & Honeysuckle

Two shrubby climbers, the jasmine and honeysuckle, have a particular claim on our attention because of their scent. They have generally been allowed to form a loose tangle against the cottage wall or to be the principals over an arbour. (Note that the fidgety, lattice-work, rustic arbours you often see are the products of a suburban mentality and that they soon collapse. The simpler the framework the better; it can be stout without looking ponderous.)

The extended natural distribution of the white-flowered common jasmine, *Jasminum officinale*, is from the Caucasus to China but it has been cultivated in Britain since at least the middle of the sixteenth century. It flowers in high summer and exhales its scent at night until the dew dries the next morning.

So, too, does the woodbine or common honeysuckle, *Lonicera periclymenum*. This is about the only flower you will see outside a West Highlands Scottish croft, probably because it has been sown from the wild by birds. There are improved garden selections, of which the late Dutch honeysuckle, *L.p.* 'Serotina', with dark red on the outside of the flower, is one of the best. It starts blooming in mid-summer and continues into autumn.

The creamy-white-flowered variety of the Japanese honeysuckle, *L. japonica* 'Halliana', is popular in Britain (but a terrible weed scourge in the United States), mainly on account of being evergreen even though its appearance in winter is shabby. The flowers often do not make a great display, but they are very heavily scented.

Wisteria & Sweet Peas

Although too vigorous for many cottage gardens, wisteria should also be mentioned. The rich mauve *Wisteria sinensis*, with comparatively short, pendent racemes of pea flowers in late spring, and quite a useful, secondary crop in late summer, is the best species for scent – a really delicious and summery fragrance. It has been cultivated in Britain since the early nineteenth century. Search out the most reliable supplier, a nurseryman with a good reputation, for your plant. It will be of the same clone as that originally introduced and vegetatively propagated ever since; it should also be of a good colour (not washed out) and start to flower regularly from an early age. This will avoid the all-too-familiar "my wisteria doesn't flower" story.

One expects to see sweet peas in any cottage garden, perhaps in a very short row, or trained up a wigwam of brushwood among other plants or even, similarly trained, in a tub close to the house. The sweet pea, *Lathyrus odoratus*, was introduced from Sicily in 1700 and the earliest ones had small, deep purplish-blue flowers.

Until early this century, Grandiflora, or giant-flowered, sweet peas ruled. Their flowers were half the size of the Spencer sweet peas that followed and their standard petal was not frilled. Grandifloras had such names as 'Striped Invincible', 'Painted Lady' (pink and white forms are still obtainable), 'Bride of Niagara' and 'Her Majesty'. They are now insignificant for show purposes but, because they have a far more powerful scent than modern sweet peas, they are still popular. In fact, they are the only kind I grow. The fashionable sweet pea is really too big and ostentatious in a cottage context unless the show bench is your goal, and there has always been a place for such a goal among cottage gardeners.

The rigmarole of growing sweet peas for show is considerable and gardeners can become fanatic about it. However, just to enjoy unassuming, yet gay,

SCENTED CLIMBER A massive honeysuckle, Lonicera periclymenum, *grows across the front of this cottage. Honeysuckles are one of the most popular of scented climbers.*

COTTAGE CLOTHING Train wisteria up the front of the cottage or an outbuilding, where it will drip with scented racemes of flowers in late spring and early summer.

scented flowers in the garden from mid-summer to mid-autumn you need not sow your seed until early to mid-spring, perhaps on a protected windowsill to get the plants started. 'Old-Fashioned Sweet-Scented' is the way most seed houses designate the Grandiflora sweet peas. They are usually listed at the end of the sweet-pea section in the catalogues.

It is only sensible at this point to include the everlasting pea, *Lathyrus grandiflorus*, which has been a staunch cottage favourite for 150 years. Usually it is seen in an obese, semi-collapsed state, trussed to the cottage wall, although it sometimes receives better treatment and certainly deserves it, being a bonny perennial climber. I've seen it in Scotland more than anywhere. The flowers are magenta and maroon, not in the least subtle, but jolly. Often mistakenly called everlasting *sweet* pea, it has no scent at all.

Shrubs

There will not be the space for many large shrubs in a cottage garden but lilac is one that should be included, preferably an unruly, suckering specimen closely akin to the unimproved species, *Syringa vulgaris*. This is the common lilac and has the best scent of all. If you're buying one of the improved cultivars, try to get one that is on its own roots. The suckers will then have the same characteristics as the main plant and not those of the wild stock, which would steadily take over if present.

Lilac is a dull and ungainly shrub when out of flower, so grow a climber or two through it, perhaps the purple *Clematis* × *jackmanii* or the hawthorn-scented *C. flammula*, with a great mass of tiny, star-like, white blossom in late summer.

The other scented clematis that you might expect to see in any cottage garden is the ultra-vigorous *C. montana*, whose white flowers smell of vanilla, or one of its scented pink forms, such as 'Elizabeth'. These flower in spring and are best seen when growing through a fruit tree or trained along a fence.

Annuals & Biennials

Mignonette, a hardy annual, is supremely grown for its scent, having rather coarse leaves and a cone of green-and-brownish flowers, more quaint than beautiful. It was beloved of Victorian cottage gardens. The basic species, *Reseda odorata,* exudes a better fragrance than any of the improved, larger-flowered kinds, and is most fragrant in sunshine.

Sweet scabious, *Scabiosa atropurpurea*, also called pincushion flower, is an annual that has gone rather out of favour. The months it takes to start flowering and its lanky habit make it unattractive commercially. But it fits perfectly into a cottage-garden jumble and is a good cut flower.

Plants with Aromatic Leaves

There are a number of aromatic plants, often evergreen, that are grown as much for the smell of their leaves as for their flowers.

Some roses, for example, exude scent from their foliage, notably the stewed-apple fragrance of sweet briar, *Rosa eglanteria* (*R. rubiginosa*). This also carries a fine display of scarlet hips and is disease-free. The Penzance briars derived from it are more colourful but they are martyrs to black spot. Other roses, such as *R. serafinii*, possess glandular stems and leaves to scent the air. *R. primula*, with wan, single, yellow flowers in late spring, justifies a place in any cottage garden with its incense fragrance, especially noticeable during and after warm rain.

Introduced into Britain at quite an early date, the sweet flag, *Acorus calamus*, has iris-like leaves. When dried or bruised, these emit a smell like cinnamon and can be strewed on floors. It is a moisture lover and the cream-variegated form is well worth including near the margin of any pool. Another plant that smells best when dried is woodruff, *Galium odoratum*, a low, creeping, shade-loving perennial with several whorls of bright green leaves and, in spring, pure white, cruciform flowers.

Lavender as a flower has been greatly improved in modern times, the rich purple *Lavandula* 'Hidcote' being probably the brightest clone today, although its foliage is not up to much. Old English lavender has grayer leaves and the strongest possible fragrance. Its pale mauve flowers are not showy and the habit of the shrub is leggy. But lavender does not have to be planted as a hedge; in a cottage garden it seldom was and nor were the bushy herbs thyme and rosemary nor box. They are more suitable as the frame to knots in upper-class gardens. Lavender can take its place and have any awkwardness in its shape masked among all sorts of plants, including annuals and perennials. The flowers are scented on the air but, generally, the plant is not.

Rosemary, too, has a gawky habit but this is one of its charms. The gnarled sprawl taken on by an old rosemary bush is most attractive and other plants can be grown between its branches. *Rosmarinus officinalis* 'Benenden Blue' has a pleasing habit – its leaves are fine and needle-like, its flowers rich-blue.

Aromatic Shrubs

Our native box, *Buxus sempervirens*, which grows wild on chalk soils, has many cultivated varieties, some vigorous, some dwarf. Generally it has been grown in cottage gardens to form clipped, ball-like specimens, perhaps a couple placed near the garden entrance or a pair either side of the front door. Box is easily trained into simple topiary shapes, such as a cottage loaf or brooding hen, but its soft texture is unsuited to elaborate topiary work and it is easily squashed out of shape by snow or children. For those who knew it when they were young, its indescribable leaf smell is remarkable for the nostalgia it evokes.

Bay laurel, *Laurus nobilis*, has been cultivated in Britain since the sixteenth century, if not earlier. The strong flavour of its leaves is excellent, in moderation, for numerous culinary purposes. Allowed to grow freely, it makes a large shrub or small tree, but it bears clipping well, where space is restricted. Clipped bays, however, are better suited to town balconies and hotel entrances than to the cottage garden and they are often attacked by scale insects. A free-growing bay flowers in late spring and wafts a most delightful scent.

LONG-LASTING FRAGRANCE You can grow fragrant sweet peas up pea sticks arranged in rows or in circular "wigwams". The cut flowers are long-lasting.

WILD PLANTS

A GREAT MANY COTTAGE-GARDEN plants were originally introduced from the wild; that was the natural and easiest thing to do. Oddities would catch the eye, like those with double flowers or unusually coloured or variegated leaves. Some people always seem to have their eyes open for such aberrations as do others for fossils or artifacts when they are turning over the soil. I myself found a George III halfpenny when cultivating my long border and spotted a purple-leaved celandine in a nearby wood which I named *Ranunculus ficaria* 'Brazen Hussy' and to which the Royal Horticultural Society subsequently gave an Award of Merit! Those such as I have eyes so constantly turned to the ground that we entirely fail to notice the name on the aeroplanes flying overhead, although we do look for the first – and last – swallows.

I have already mentioned a good many wild flowers earlier in the chapter, in other contexts, but I shall gather some more together here, as well as a few, such as evening primrose, which, although not actual natives, have made themselves very much at home both in the wild and in cultivation. Often they reach our gardens first and then escape.

Hedges

The framework of a cottage garden is, traditionally, a wall in the north of Britain and other mountainous areas but generally a hedge of hawthorn or quickthorn (or, for short, just quick) in the lowlands. Hawthorn has many advantages. Although not evergreen, it makes a dense, cattle-proof and windproof hedge. Furthermore, its bright green leaf buds are visible in earliest spring, so it is much more cheerful during that season than beech or hornbeam, which hang on to their dead leaves and rustle rather dismally. Hawthorn grows fast (hurrah!) but needs clipping twice a year (boo!).

NATURAL SETTING Hedgerows are the natural place to grow wild flowers, whether at the bottom of the hedge or like this sweet-scented wild honeysuckle, Lonicera periclymenum, *climbing through the hedge itself.*

A GARDEN ESCAPE Many wild flowers are happy growing on walls. Here Corydalis ochroleuca, *a naturalized garden escape, looks perfectly at home.*

Privet is another common cottage-garden hedging material, although the Japanese *Ligustrum ovalifolium* has replaced our native *L. vulgare*, because it holds some of its leaves for longer, although the appeal of that is doubtful. A half-furnished hedge of glum, green, oval leaves is not inspiring during the short, dark days of winter. Grown as a shrub and pruned only occasionally, green or golden privet is super, flowering well and setting heavy trusses of handsome black berries, which go particularly well with the pink and orange fruits of spindle, *Euonymus europaeus*.

Yew, *Taxus baccata*, is the quality hedging material, the ideal background to anything you care to name, and it requires clipping only once a year. If this is done in late summer it will hold its shape into the following spring. Not many genuine cottage gardens are hedged with yew – it has been used more often for the occasional topiary piece.

Hops, *Humulus lupulus*, will readily clamber over a roughish hedge or else a length of fence. The attractive swags of cone-shaped fruits on a female hop give a wonderful feeling of autumn bounty and their sharp, astringent smell is tremendously satisfying. The golden hop, with its lime-green foliage, is a great asset, too.

Shrubs

The bay willow, *Salix pentandra*, is often grown along boundaries in north Scotland and Orkney. Any shrub over 6ft (180cm) high qualifies as a tree in those windy parts, and the bay willow attains a little more height than that. Glossy, bright green young leaves in late spring and early summer coincide with the vivid yellow pussies on the male bushes, so be sure you have a male plant.

In Scotland, of course, you would expect to see heathers in most gardens. The prototypes, after all, grow wild in the highlands: ling, *Calluna vulgaris*, the bell heathers, *Erica cinerea* and cross-leaved heath, *E. tetralix*, which is a soft shade of pink and grows well in boggy places. These, by selection, have been greatly "improved" (at least in the opinion of some). In lowland gardens, however, heathers tend to look rather silly and misplaced.

In areas where butcher's broom, *Ruscus aculeatus*, grows wild, generally on lime-rich soils, it will often be found in nearby gardens. This fiercely prickly, evergreen shrub, usually no more than 2ft (60cm) high, is an excellent deterrent to anyone cutting corners. A woodlander, it will tolerate shade, even dry shade.

Spring Flowers

*Early colour in the garden is primarily composed of pastels,
which give the feeling of a soft, fresh appearance.*

❖ *ALYSSUM* (Alyssum saxatile)
*Racemes of tiny, vivid yellow flowers
completely cover this bushy, evergreen,
clump-forming perennial. Prefers full sun
and well-drained soil.*

❖ *BLEEDING HEART* (Dicentra
spectabilis) *Heart-shaped, pinkish-red
and white flowers and fern-like foliage
grace this herbaceous perennial. Prefers
partial shade and well-drained soil.*

❖ *LILAC* (Syringa *x* persica) *This
variety of the deciduous shrub produces
fragrant purple flowers. White, yellow,
pink and carmine varieties are available.
Prefers full sun and well-drained soil.*

❖ *WOOD ANEMONES* (Anemone
nemorosa) *This carpeting, rhizomatous
perennial from the woods bears flat,
star-shaped flowers in several colours.
Prefers partial shade and moist soil.*

❖ *OXSLIP* (Primula elatior) *Umbels
of delicate, fragrant, tubular yellow flowers
appear on this rare, British-native, clump-
forming perennial. Prefers partial shade
and moist soil.*

❖ *FLOWERING CURRANT* (Ribes
sanguineum *'Pulborough Scarlet'*) *This
shrub bears pendent, deep red flowers amid
aromatic foliage. Prefers full sun and
well-drained soil.*

It has a dark and sombre presence, although you must clean out spent branches to keep it smart. The fruits are crimson-red but seldom seen because each shrub is either male or female – a female berry-bearer requires a male for pollination and the two sexes are rarely found growing together except in the wild. But there is a hermaphrodite form that comes true from seed. With both sexes on the same plant you are assured of handsome berry crops.

Butcher's broom looks well with the stinking *Iris foetidissima*, which enjoys the same alkaline conditions and also fruits in autumn with bright orange seeds.

The spurge laurel, *Daphne laureola*, has rosettes of glossy evergreen leaves on a 3ft (90cm) shrub, which grows wild in woodland on basic soils. Its night-scented, green flowers appear early in the year, should you be out at the right time to sniff them.

The other daphne that must be mentioned is mezereon, *Daphne mezereum*, which is native to limestone woodland. When I was a schoolboy, I found it in Ufton Wood in Warwickshire, but whether or not it was a garden escape is hard to say, since birds certainly scatter its seed around generously. On the pinky-mauve-flowered species of the plant the berries are red; on the white form, yellow. The scent, during early to mid-spring, is terrific. In sophisticated gardens where disease is more prevalent mezereon is liable to succumb, whereas in a cottage garden it will grow larger and bonnier for years and years.

----- *Woodland Plants* -----

A great many woodlanders are cottage-garden favourites, no doubt because the British Isles were once covered by a good deal of woodland. Primroses and anemones have already been mentioned, although it should be added that bunch primroses, or polyanthus, were developed by cottagers and artisans as were the laced varieties, in which a dark flower is edged with yellow.

In the wild, sweet violets, *Viola odorata*, are less often found in deep woodland than in scrub, where there is a good deal of light in early spring and where they can nestle under any deciduous shrub or hedge for shelter from excess wind and sun. Typically their flowers are violet or white but there are also pink and pale apricot-yellow varieties. Neither are the odourless violets, of which *Viola riviniana* is the commonest, to be despised. They flower a little later, in late spring, and make pools of mauve. In my garden they self-sow in paving cracks.

VIGOROUS WILD FLOWER One of the best wild plants to introduce is the foxglove, Digitalis purpurea. *Remove the seedheads to prevent excessive self-sowing.*

Lady's smock or cuckoo flower, *Cardamine pratensis*, is best grown in its double-flowered form, which is of ancient lineage. The flowers are pale mauve borne in neat rosettes like a miniature stock.

Red campion, *Silene dioica*, is lovely at bluebell time. Its double form lasts in flower for a long while and is widely grown in Scotland. The Shetland variety, *S. zetlandicum*, found also in Orkney, is more intensely coloured and grows wild on the sea cliffs. Cottagers often include it in their gardens. The foxglove, *Digitalis purpurea*, is another woodland perennial that tends to grow in open places in Scotland. You also see it on the shingle at Dungeness in Kent. Pure white forms occur frequently in the wild, sometimes predominating over the pink, but there are many selected seed strains to choose from for the cottage garden.

Cottage Favourites

Many of the flowers we see in our gardens are derived from wild plants. Cottagers had a keen eye for spotting anything that was attractive or different. As well as deliberate introductions, wild plants often entered the cottage garden of their own volition, particularly along the bottoms of hedges.

MEADOW CRANESBILL (Geranium pratense) *This wild flower has long been a favourite in cottage gardens and is still widely grown. You often see its double form. The leaves are also attractive, taking on good autumn colour.*

TEASEL (Dipsacus fullonum) *This statuesque, spiny plant with its intriguingly shaped flowers is very attractive to bees. It is also good for drying.*

BLACKBERRY (Rubus fruticosus) *Although tolerated in the hedgerow more for their fruit than their flowers, the flowers do look very cottagey.*

EVERLASTING PEA (Lathyrus latifolius) *Unlike the sweet pea, the everlasting pea is odourless. It is nevertheless a valuable, bold, scrambling plant for the border. A perennial usually seen bearing pink flowers, the white form is more beautiful.*

PURPLE LOOSESTRIFE (Lythrum salicaria) *Commonly found in damp areas beside streams or ponds, cultivated forms of loosestrife have been developed and there are now several good varieties available, all with strong spikes of purple flowers.*

MEADOWSWEET
(Filipendula ulmaria)
A common sight in wetter places
about the countryside, its
frothy heads are made of
tiny cream flowers, which
are very strongly
scented. This plant is
ideal for planting near
a pond.

JACOB'S LADDER
(Polemonium
caeruleum)
This familiar
plant usually
has blue or sometimes,
as here, white flowers
in early summer.

WELSH POPPY
(Meconopsis cambrica)
This variety of
poppy sows itself
around the garden
with gay
abandon.

VIPER'S BUGLOSS
(Echium vulgare)
This biennial should
have a place in any border,
in spite of being a wildling.
It has handsome spikes
of intense blue flowers,
which are much
loved by bees.

WILD-FLOWER
POSY Wild flowers
can make a delightful
posy that retains the
freshness and simplicity
of the countryside.

COMMON TOADFLAX
(Linaria vulgaris) This
attractive wild flower of the roadside
verges has a tendency
to run.

IVY-LEAVED TOADFLAX
(Cymbalaria muralis) Walls
and rocks are the common
home for this attractive wild
flower, which seems to
introduce itself from nowhere.
The plant usually has
purple flowers but
there is an albino
form as well.

Plants from other Habitats

A mountain and sea-cliff flower that you often see cultivated in Scotland is rose root, *Rhodiola rosea* (*Sedum rosea*). Above glaucous foliage, it carries heads of lime-green flowers and is often mistaken for a spurge. There are male and female plants, but both are handsome. On sea cliffs it often grows alongside white sea campion, *Silene maritima*, of which the double form is preferred in cottage gardens. You might also see it with the white, pink and purple shades of viper's bugloss, *Echium vulgare*.

Closely related is snow-in-summer, *Cerastium tomentosum*, which forms huge grey mats mantled with a duvet of white blossom in early summer. It is an invasive plant but looks just right in a certain type of stony, seaside garden. Although no native, it has naturalized widely. In the Orkney island of Westray it looked dramatic as an outer frame to a cottager's planting of lupins, the deep blue, anchusa-like *Cynoglossum nervosum* (more popular and vigorous in Scotland than further south) and sweet rocket.

Globe flowers, *Trollius europaeus*, are often introduced from the wild into cottage gardens, especially in northern Britain, where they flourish in wet places. Their cheerful, yellow flowers boast incurved petals.

Columbines, *Aquilegia vulgaris*, may occur in open woodland or in meadowland on wood fringes. Their range of colour is not as extensive as their long-spurred relatives (which would also be quite at home in a cottage garden), but they cover some pretty shades of blue, mauve, old rose, purple and white. Beware of them – they are inveterate self-seeders. They may be very pretty in flower but they will leave you with a scene of dereliction later.

Jacob's ladder, *Polemonium caeculeum*, with its lavender or white flowers comes from the Pennines and looks purpose-made for cottage gardens.

The musk or monkey flower, *Mimulus moschatus*, with its yellow-and-orange-spotted flowers, is jolly and unrefined. There is no nonsense either with evening primroses, *Oenothera*, the biennial kinds of which have yellow flowers that open in a series of jerks at sunset. Both *O. biennis*, a somewhat stringy plant, and the big, branching, 6ft (180cm) tall *O. erythrosepala* are naturalized on dunes around Britain's coasts. I saw a hedge of the latter behind a wall in a Cotswold garden, one drizzly summer's morning. Because of the weather, they showed no signs of wilting and the display was amazing.

Of meadow flowers, two cranesbills have become popular cottage-garden plants with a number of selected clones. The blue meadow cranesbill, *Geranium pratense*, is scarcely in need of improvement, though its albino, stripy-flowered and double, blue and purple forms are all worth cultivating. The bloody cranesbill, *G. sanguineum*, generally growing near the sea, has been selected for its most vivid colouring, as has an albino (rather a thin flower) and the pale pink *G.s.* var. *striatum* (*G.s.* var. *lancastriense*).

The harebell (or bluebell in Scotland, where England's bluebell is known as the wild hyacinth), *Campanula rotundifolia*, is often found in cottage gardens in northern Britain, where it also abounds in the wild. One of its happiest sites is the short turf that sometimes caps an old stone wall. Here, also, you will find the lady's bedstraw, *Galium verum*, with its loose panicles of cheerful yellow flowers.

POPULAR WILD FLOWER Granny's bonnet, Aquilegia vulgaris, has always been a popular wild flower.

Another campanula that moves in and out of gardens from the wild, especially in northern England (I associate it with high summer in Derbyshire and Yorkshire) is the tall and stately *Campanula latifolia*. A hedgerow and roadside plant by nature, it makes a good companion for foxgloves. Its flowers are most often a pale greyish-white, but the most desirable forms are rich campanula-purple. Found wild on chalk downland is the invasive *C. glomerata* with its deep violet-purple flowers. Try an improved variety, such as *C.g.* 'Superba' in the garden.

COMPLEMENTING NEIGHBOURS *The native harebell,* Campanula rotundiflora, *grows here with French lavender,* Lavandula stoechas.

BRITISH NATIVE *Originally from Europe, masterwort,* Astrantia major, *has established itself as a British native.*

ANNUALS & BIENNIALS

OF THE DIFFERENT CATEGORIES of annual, those that are hardy and can be sown in *situ*, often self-sowing thereafter, have played an important part in the cottage garden. Half-hardy annuals have taken on a much lesser role, because they need the protection of a windowsill or greenhouse in the winter.

Today, with a large bedding-plant industry and numerous garden-centre outlets, there is no reason why anyone should deprive themselves of petunias, begonias, impatiens and all the other tender bedders treated as annuals (although most of them are technically perennials). As cottage-garden plants, their place is in history today rather than yesterday. I shall therefore concentrate on flowers of a more traditional type – most of which are hardy.

Hardy Annuals

Nasturtium, *Tropaeolum majus*, could be described as a hardy annual, for even though it succumbs to the first frosts of autumn you can push its seeds into the ground where you wish them to develop and they will germinate at quite low temperatures. Self-sown nasturtium seedlings will often appear in mid-winter if it is mild. For the most relaxed effect they must be of climbing habit rather than upright, which all nasturtiums originally were.

Climbers, when they have nothing to climb up or over, become trailers and that looks good too, as in Monet's cottage-style garden at Giverny, where they sprawl across the paths. Their hot colours show up in shade and they grow excellently against a shady fence or hedge, preferably in moist conditions. They are no less satisfying when garlanding a garden rubbish heap. Gourds, too, are suitable for this purpose: gourds, marrows, ridge cucumbers, and squashes, – whether edible or not – are decorative when flinging themselves around with incredible luxuriance, during the warmest months of the year. The fact that you never quite know which way they'll explore next adds to the hilarious mayhem. Suddenly, one morning, a great yellow star of a marrow flower greets you from the lower branches of an apple tree. All you can do is bow and say "good morning".

NATIVE PERENNIAL Musk mallow,
Malva moschata, *with its lightly
scented leaves, is a native short-lived
perennial treated as a biennial.*

OLD FAVOURITES Snapdragons,
Antirrhinum majus, *are attractive,
easy-to-grow annuals that have
retained their popularity for generations
with both children and adults.*

*BLUE EYE-CATCHER (right) Forget-
me-nots,* Myosotis sylvatica, *with
their blue flowers, are eye-catching
wherever they appear.*

Cottage Favourites

Annuals and biennials have always played an important part in the cottage garden, particularly the self-sowing kind. In the past the cottager did not have much time for raising plants afresh each year, but the attractive and brilliant colours have ensured that a few were raised every spring. Make your selection carefully so that they fit in with the cottage garden.

FORGET-ME-NOT (*Myosotis alpestris*) *Once introduced, this plant will happily sow itself around the garden.*

TOBACCO PLANT (*Nicotiana alata*) *This straggly annual is much appreciated for its evening scent, a quality that many modern colour strains lack. It will sometimes self-sow, but not enough to become a nuisance.*

OPIUM POPPY (*Papaver somniferum*) *This variety of poppy (below) also perpetuates itself. There are several different colour forms as well as shaggy doubles.*

SNAPDRAGON (*Antirrhinum majus*) *This plant of our childhood is a firm cottage-garden favourite. There are now a wide range of colours and heights available.*

NASTURTIUM (Tropaeolum majus)
*Valuable plants, nasturtiums
provide a vivid splash of colour
towards the end of the year
when the garden can look
a bit tired. They can be
used as climbers or as
ground cover to fill spaces
when other plants have
finished flowering. The
colours vary from bright
reds to yellows.*

GARDEN PANSY (Viola x
wittrockiana) *With its
cheeky face, the pansy
has been grown in
cottage gardens for
generations. It was
once one of the main
florists' flowers, grown for
show and competitions. If
cut back, many will last for
more than one year.*

LOVE-IN-A-MIST (Nigella
damascena) *With such an
alluring common
name, this
annual must be
delightful and it is.
The blue
flowers float
amongst feathery
leaves and bracts,
finally forming
attractive, inflated
seed cases.*

CORNFLOWER
(Centaurea cyanus)
*Once regarded
as the weed of the
cornfields, this annual
is now grown for its
magnificent blue
flowers. Other
coloured strains are
now available but the
blue is still the one to grow.*

FOXGLOVE (Digitalis
purpurea) *These plants
are a must. The flowers
on the wild varieties all
face the same way and
are either purple or white.
Modern, cultivated forms
come in a larger range of
colours and with flowers all
around the stems. They are
vigorous self-sowers.*

Adaptable Favourites

The sky-blue morning glory, *Ipomoea tricolor*, needs to be started in a pot on a warm windowsill and then transferred to a trellis against the cottage, where it will catch every scrap of sunshine. Morning glory hates cold nights, so sow in late spring and leave it in its pot as it flowers better when its roots are confined. Apply liquid fertilizer while it is growing strongly to help with flowering. A hot summer also helps. Its colour, shading to white at the centre, is exquisite.

If, in or around your cottage garden, there are walls rather than fences, let us hope the mortar in them is rotten or that there is no mortar, just rubble. Then you could grow snapdragons, not just as annuals but showing their perenniality in these well-drained positions that they so love. Sometimes, where the wall is solid and well rendered, it can be capped with mud and clay, thereby allowing the snapdragons, or wallflowers, to make a frieze along the top. Besides the common wallflower, *Cheiranthus cheiri*, the Siberian kind, *C. allionii* (*Erysimum perowskianum*) is a great self-sower and its brilliant orange colouring looks most welcoming, haphazardly scattered around rather than bedded out in neat but indigestible blocks.

That, also, is the way I like forget-me-nots – self-sown. They may not be as intense a blue as those grown from a packet, but they never deteriorate over the years to the extent that you would remark "my forget-me-nots aren't blue enough".

Cultivated Weeds

Love-in-a-mist, *Nigella damascena*, should be blue it seems to me. *N.d.* 'Miss Jekyll' is that colour, and will retain its purity if you eschew the other shades. So long as you keep your garden cultivated, love-in-a-mist will return annually from its own seed, the largest seedlings developing from those that germinated in autumn and grew through the winter months.

Cornflowers, *Centaurea cyanus*, have a similar growth pattern. In the wild they are always blue but I must admit to enjoying some of the other colours now available – pink, white and maroon, especially. Given good soil and plenty of space, they will grow 4–5ft (120–150cm) tall and need support, so the dwarf strains may be more convenient.

With larkspurs, derived from *Delphinium consolida* and *D. ajacis*, the tall, branching plants are much the most impressive and the best for cut flowers. They last for ages in water, retaining much of their beauty even when the petals have dried. Curiously, although quite unrelated to cornflowers, their colour range is similar, apart from wild larkspurs which are violet coloured, never pure blue. I remember, on the Hungarian plains one early summer, seeing a field of violet-blue larkspurs stretching in laminated streaks from my feet to the horizon. They were, like the cornflower, a weed of cultivation that has entirely disappeared from farmland where selective weed-killers are used as a matter of routine.

Corn cockle, *Agrostemma githago*, originally from the Mediterranean but widely naturalized in British cornfields, is a proud, upstanding plant, rooting deeply and bearing magenta-coloured, circular flowers, 2in (5cm) across. The seeds are poisonous and will spoil a sample of wheat flour, so we should not shed too many tears that it is seldom seen in cornfields now. The variety *A.g.* 'Milas', with 3in- (7.5cm-) wide flowers, is a splendid annual, excellent as a pot-grown specimen (with one supporting cane) as well as in the cottage garden where it makes up for the loss in the wild.

Then there is the corn marigold, *Chrysanthemum segetum*, with its rich, butter-yellow daisies. Although now gone from cornfields, you can still see it wild in parts of Scotland and Ireland. It is, in fact, an introduction, although it looks at home with a background of Scottish hills. I love it, since it does me no harm. There are "improved" garden seed strains, including doubles, but none with the intense simplicity of the wild plant.

Many of our other beautiful cornfield weeds have now disappeared, but it is no use being sentimental about their demise; the farmer needs to make his living and can do so more easily without weeds than with them. That is a price of civilization. We can still buy these "weeds" for our gardens in seed packets, paying for the privilege.

Field Poppies

The beauty of field poppies in flower makes you catch your breath. Often when farmland, long left uncultivated, is brought into a new road-widening operation the ground is disturbed and gives dormant poppy seeds their chance of germination. Suddenly they appear in thousands, a brilliant scarlet stain mixed, perhaps with the yellow of charlock. These field poppies will be *Papaver rhoeas* or, more commonly in Northern Britain, the long-headed poppy,

Early Summer Flowers

The cottage garden is a riotous mass of blooms by early summer, blazing in every colour under the sun.

❖ *Sweet Pea* (Lathyrus odoratus 'Knee Hi') *This fast-growing annual is loved for its highly fragrant flowers in shades of pink, red, blue or white. Prefers full sun and well-drained soil.*

❖ *Peony* (Paeonia) *These exotic, luxuriant flowers can be single, double or anemone-form and bloom in white, yellows, pinks and reds. Prefers full sun and well-drained soil.*

❖ *Lady's Mantle* (Alchemilla mollis) *Sprays of tiny, bright, greenish-yellow flowers embellish this rampant groundcover. Prefers partial shade and well-drained soil.*

❖ *Old-fashioned Pink* (Dianthus 'White Ladies') *Masses of fragrant flowers crown this evergreen, clump-forming perennial wih silvery foliage. Prefers full sun and well-drained soil.*

❖ *Double Daisies* (Bellis perennis) *A slow-growing, carpeting perennial grown as a biennial with small, daisy-like double flowers in white, pink or red. Prefers full sun and well-drained soil.*

❖ *Stock* (Matthiola) *Long spikes tower over lance-shaped leaves and are smothered in highly scented flowers in shades of pink, red, pale blue and white. Prefers full sun and well-drained soil.*

P. dubium which has an elongated rather than a globose seed pod and paler scarlet flowers. Shirley poppies, which belong so firmly to cottage gardens, derive from *P. rhoeas* and grow in a beautiful and varied range of colours. If you allow them to keep on self-sowing through the years, however, they will revert to scarlet. Some people, disliking bright colours, select from pastel shades, but their flower colours will never be fixed entirely.

Opium Poppies

Even commoner in cottage gardens is the self-perpetuating opium poppy, *P. somniferum*, with its glaucous foliage. The flowers are typically single and mauve, with a purple basal blotch, but by selection there exist some wonderfully coloured, often double varieties (called carnation-flowered or peony-flowered in the catalogues). They grow to 3½ft

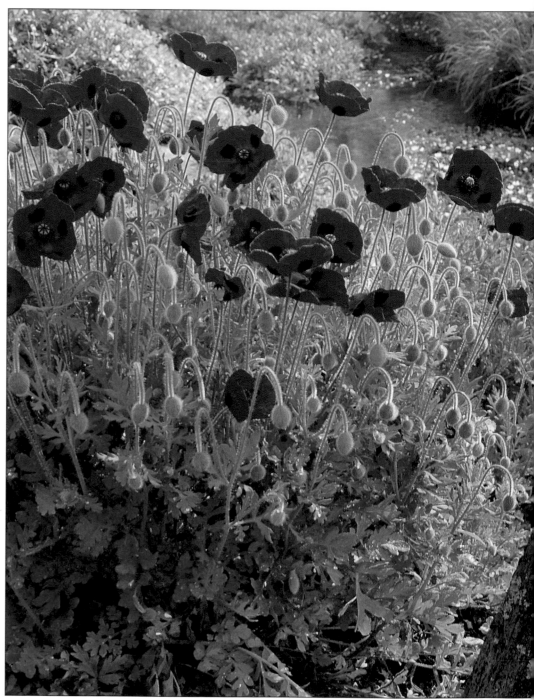

ABUNDANT SELF-SOWER The opium poppy, Papaver somniferum, *is an abundant self-sower that produces both single and shaggy double flowers in shades of red, pink, purple and white as well as decorative seedheads, which you can dry for indoor decoration.*

FLEETING BRILLIANCE Poppies can produce a red flower that is rarely matched by other plants. However, its brilliance is fleeting as each flower is short-lived. Poppies are vigorous self-sowers, often popping up in the most unexpected places, or in drifts like the Papaver commutatum *shown here.*

(105cm) in the garden and also look good if you allow their knob-like seedheads to develop. They are likely to be removed though – anything knob-like being irresistible to adults as well as children, who have to clutch it and break it off. Although opium poppies have a tendency to revert to the rather uninteresting, single-flowered species plant, many of the seedlings will continue to be double and/or handsomely coloured through the years.

Poppies are easy to grow but one thing they hate is being transplanted. They should always be sown in *situ* and thinned as necessary. Opium poppies have such smooth leaves that they attract and hold large water drops, whether of rain or dew. They are, with chickweed, the wettest and messiest plants to weed among that I know.

Californian & Horned Poppies

The related Californian poppies, *Eschscholzia*, make sprawling plants with divided leaves and bright orange flowers, and may often be seen on wasteland and roadsides in California, daringly combined with bright pink clarkias. They are happiest on light, sandy soils, where they may often survive the winter and start flowering again in late spring. There are some glamorous seed strains, including pinks and reds and double flowers, but they all revert by self-sowing to single orange flowers over the years, and that is the way you will generally see them in cottage gardens. It is the way I like them, too.

There is another poppy I should like to mention, particularly suitable for stony soil, especially near the coast where it grows wild. This is the horned poppy, *Glaucium flavum*. It has beautiful bluish basal leaves with rippling margins and yellow flowers on 3ft (90cm) stems; each flower lasts only a day but then matures into a long, horn-shaped pod.

Working with Nature

Sometimes it is not a bad idea to accept flowers as they were intended by Mother Nature. Take ageratums, for instance. Something near to the wild species is still obtainable, growing 2ft (60cm) tall and of a free and easy habit. It is useful for cutting and is a satisfying shade of lavender that contrasts well with bronzy marigolds. I far prefer its unbuttoned look to the tight little 4–6in (10–15cm) globes with which many gardeners like to edge their paths and borders.

Together with horned poppies on shingle beaches – and you might well take a hint from Nature – you will see the viper's bugloss, *Echium vulgare*, a member of the borage family, with upright spikes of blue flowers. This species is generally biennial but the echium more commonly cultivated is *E. plantagineum*, a bushy, hardy annual that grows up to 1½ft (45cm) tall. The pale blue strain, 'Blue Bedder' is my favourite but the mixture of blue, pink and white in the species has its own charm. These are great self-seeders on light soils, including chalk.

The annual sage, *Salvia horminum*, has a similar colour range to viper's bugloss (although purple takes the place of blue). With this it is the top-knot of bracts that makes the display – the flowers are inconspicuous. It is a shame that this plant should so often be mis-named 'clary', a name that obviously belongs to the biennial sage, *S. sclarea*, grown in gardens as the variety *turkestanica*. Both its pale mauve flowers and the pinkish-mauve bracts look well, but best of all is its upstanding, branching habit to 4ft (120cm). I always remember *S. sclarea* in the way I once saw it growing: along the top of a wall that divided a cottage garden on its higher level from the road beneath. The plant has an extremely pungent aroma that takes some getting used to.

You might expect to see sunflowers, *Helianthus annuus*, in a similar position, or else peering over the top of a hedge. The huge disc at the centre of its yellow rays ripens into the oil-rich seeds that make it such a valuable crop in warm countries. Grow the double-flowered variants for a change. Sunflowers are, of course, very attractive to children who love watching their staggering growth.

Cruciferous Flowers

Another vigorous grower, but on a smaller scale, is the Virginian stock, *Malcomia maritima*. Its pink, mauve or white cruciferous flowers, on each 6–9in (15–23cm) plant, are pretty for ephemeral edgings. This annual develops quickly from seed to flower.

Several more of the four-petalled plants in the family *Cruciferae* could appropriately claim our attention. Sweet alyssum, *Lobularia maritima*, for example, is now available in a range of pink and mauve shades, although typically white, and is sweetly scented. Its cushions make it popular for edging, but I like it even better between paving cracks, where it self-sows. Another such relative is the 3in- (7.5cm-) high violet cress, *Ionopsidium acaule*, which has white flowers with a tinge of mauve. It is good in a damp, shady spot where it readily self-sows, if happy.

Annual candytuft, *Iberis*, is delightful when not starved, and produces flowers in shades of magenta, rosy-purple, pink, mauve and white. It grows up to 1ft (30cm) tall. A narrow border at the foot of a white paling fence, or one near a window or a seat close to the house, is an ideal situation for this fragile-looking, night-scented annual. Its flowers are in a state of collapse by day but expand with the cooler breath of evening and exhale their pungent almond fragrance.

SKY-HIGH BLOOMS *Tall plants have always had their place in the cottage garden, often brightening the side of the cottage or, as here, peering over the garden wall or fence.* Hollyhocks, Alcea rosea, *and yellow mulleins,* Verbascum, *are two favourites for this kind of position.*

There is one hardy annual that should be mentioned on account of its long history as a cottager's favourite, although I have never grown it myself and probably never shall. This is love-lies-bleeding, *Amaranthus caudatus*, which grew in gardens in Britain in Elizabethan times. Its long, rat's-tail inflorescences appear in what is nowadays generally considered a difficult colour – magenta. I do not find it in any way a problem, but I dislike this plant's coarse foliage, which the flowers do nothing to conceal. There is also a green-flowered variant that contrasts well with the magenta.

Late Summer Flowers

At the height of summer, the cottage garden is a spectacular wash of colour with each plant trying to outshine its neighbour.

❖ *HELIOPSIS* (Heliopsis *'Ballet Dancer'*) *This popular perennial is recognized by its sunny yellow, self-supporting flower heads with frilled petals. Prefers full sun and well-drained soil.*

❖ *DAY LILY* (Hemerocallis fulva) *On this vigorous clump-forming perennial each bloom lasts just one day but is replaced with a succession of new blooms. Prefers full sun and moist soil.*

❖ *SNAPDRAGON* (Antirrhinum *'Doubloon'*) *A perennial favourite with children, with flowers in white, pink, red, purple, yellow and orange. Prefers full sun and well-drained soil.*

❖ *SUNFLOWER* (Helianthus annuus *'Taiyo'*) *This giant of an annual has long been a favourite with its large, daisy-like yellow flowers and large black centres. Prefers full sun and well-drained soil.*

❖ *NASTURTIUM* (Tropaeolum majus) *This twining, bushy annual with trumpet-shaped, spurred flowers comes in glowing, jewel-like colours. Prefers full sun and well-drained soil.*

❖ *SNEEZEWORT* (Achillea ptarmica) *A quickly spreading, upright perennial that is wreathed in large heads of small, pompon-like, white flowers. Prefers full sun and well-drained soil.*

BEE & BUTTERFLY PLANTS

AT ONE TIME THE BEEHIVE provided an important and nutritious addition to the cottager's diet – honey. The keeping of bees is now thought to be too demanding by most people, quite aside from whether they are allergic to bee stings. But a modern cottager need not despair; he can assist, even if only in a small way, by ensuring that his garden plants are attractive to bees, and there is the added bonus that there is satisfaction in seeing bees at work on your flowers. The general notion that bees are "a good thing" is still widespread and it embraces wild bees.

Bumble bees, perhaps because they are heavier and more windproof, are out in much rougher weather than honey bees; they also start foraging much earlier in the day and continue later. They can be seen working on newly opened nicotiana flowers in the evening before the night moths are out and about. Bumble bees are enterprising, too. I watch them feeding in a patch of border phloxes outside my kitchen window. They are too heavy to approach a flower from the front, so they hang on further back, where the plant gives greater support, then perforate the flower tube and reach the nectar by this short cut.

Nectar is mainly stored by bees and converted into honey, while the pollen, which they store in sacs on their legs, is collected to feed the larval brood. Crocuses are an early source of pollen, and so is pussy willow or palm, *Salix caprea*, which flowers in early spring. It is not uncommon to see a male plant growing in a cottage garden.

There are certain plants that seem to be besieged by bees, mainly because the flowers themselves are densely congregated as in the stonecrops, *Sedum*, or the disc of daisy flowers. Most of those that flower by day and are not, like catkin bearers and grasses, wind-pollinated, are also visited by bees. Even the inconspicuously green-flowered *Celastrus* and its close relation *Euonymus* (which includes the spindle berries) are enthusiastically sought by the bees.

Most flowers can, therefore, be considered bee plants. Members of the family *Labiatae*, which includes thyme, mint, marjoram and bugle, are especially popular but I was intrigued that when my grey-leaved *Ballota pseudodictamnus* was flowering – quite inconspicuously to human eyes – it was besieged by one species of wild bumble bee (I am too ignorant to say which) with an orange band across the abdomen.

My *Hydrangea villosa*, a blue-flowered lacecap with plenty of fertile blossom, is visited by honey bees so single-mindedly, that their pollen sacs are themselves blue; after working in the same way on mignonette, they are bright orange.

Members of the family *Rosaceae*, which includes all the fruit blossom, are mainly the prerequisite of bees. However, I was greatly impressed one early summer's day in Argyll, Scotland, when the sweet-scented bird cherries, *Prunus padus*, with their pendent flower racemes, were besieged by Green-veined White butterflies. In autumn, when pear fruits lie rotting on the ground, we all know how intoxicated the Red Admirals become.

A FEAST FOR BUTTERFLIES Butterflies find the nectar of the honey scented summer-flowering Buddleia davidii *irresistible. It comes as no surprise that its common name is the butterfly bush.*

AUTUMN COLOUR Sedums are attractive plants to both bees and butterflies. Sedum spectabile, *seen here just coming into flower, is one of the best, giving the autumn border colour and life.*

Summer Bulbs

Most people think of bulbs only for spring but there are many exotic bulbs that bloom through the summer months.

❖ *DAHLIA* (Dahlia *'Easter Sunday'*) *Thousands of dahlias are available in a wide range of colours and shapes. This variety is a collerette form. Prefers full sun and well-drained soil.*

❖ *GLADIOLUS* (Gladiolus *'Inca Queen'*) *Long, densely packed spikes of funnel-shaped flowers range from soft pastels to vibrant pinks and reds. Prefers full sun and well-drained soil.*

❖ *ALSTROEMERIA* (Alstroemeria Ligtu Hybrids) *A tuber with widely flared flowers in shades of pink, yellow or orange are often spotted with contrasting colours. Prefers full sun and well-drained soil.*

❖ *GIANT ALLIUM* (Allium christophii) *An umbel of 50 or more star-shaped, purplish-violet flowers appears on this perennial, which dries well. Prefers full sun and well-drained soil.*

❖ *MADONNA LILY* (Lilium candidum) *The cool white of these graceful, fragrant flowers adds an elegant touch to the cottage garden. Prefers full sun and well-drained soil.*

❖ *MONTBRETIA* (Crocosmia masonorum) *The cheerful sight of the bright orangish-red flowers of this clump-forming corm brightens any odd corner. Prefers full sun and well-drained soil.*

Butterflies

Butterflies are interested solely in nectar, to maintain their strength, so they will only visit the same flowers as bees when their interests coincide. An obvious instance of converging interest is on the butterfly bush, *Buddleia davidii*. As we ourselves can easily detect this flower's honeyed scent, it is not surprising that the butterflies are attracted to it. The early summer-flowering *B. alternifolia* and the mid-autumn *B. auriculata*, although just as sweet, are only occasionally seen with a butterfly on them, which is odd and not entirely explained by there being fewer butterflies around during those seasons.

FOR BEES AND BUTTERFLIES The densely packed flowers of sedums, particularly those that flower later in the year, are favourites of bees and butterflies. This Sedum spathulifolium *'Capa Blanca' has a white powder on its fleshy leaves and yellow flowers.*

In my garden one of the most popular flowers with butterflies is the tall, to me scentless, purple *Verbena bonariensis*. Other verbenas, including most of the bedding types, are very sweetly scented, yet disregarded by butterflies.

In earliest spring, when the Peacock, Tortoiseshell and Comma are around, aubrieta is a favourite food plant; by mid-spring the Comma may have moved on to *Daphne mezereum* – a colour clash that would set any sensitive person's teeth on edge.

A cottage-garden flower famous for its butterfly-enticing properties is the ice plant, *Sedum spectabile*, with its platforms of densely packed pink blossom in late summer. The hybrid *S.* 'Autumn Joy', with a longer season, is popular with bees, but not with butterflies, in southern England. In the north, however, the butterflies are still attracted to it.

Most members of the family *Compositae*, the daisy tribe, are popular with butterflies (and bees), and this becomes increasingly evident in late summer and autumn, when they crowd upon Michaelmas daisies, dahlias, eupatoriums and perennial sunflowers.

In my garden the flower that attracts the most butterflies is *Escallonia bifida*, a moderately hardy shrub with scented, star-shaped, white blossom on which colourful butterflies show up spectacularly.

The Benefits of Insects

It has to be admitted that we only enjoy insects on our own terms. Few people, even cottagers, are prepared to grow stinging nettles as the food plant of Tortoiseshell, Red Admiral and Peacock butterflies. Neither are they pleased to see Large White and Small White butterflies, generally grouped together as Cabbage Whites, laying their eggs on cabbages, seakale, stocks and nasturtiums – all food plants for the caterpillars.

If an insect is beautiful or recognizably "useful", all well and good. But what of the wasps, which kill and feed to their young many of the larvae that would otherwise be consuming our plants? We are blind to these assets because they are invisible. What we do notice is that wasps plague us for a share of our food and drink and that they sting if we handle them roughly. So, when we see queen wasps feeding (with the bees) on *Cotoneaster horizontalis* blossom in late spring, why is our thought to catch and kill, rather than stand back indulgently and watch? If you train yourself to be more tolerant and to restrain yourself as a spectator, life becomes richer in its interests.

Cottage Favourites

The busy drone of the bee and the airy flitting of the butterfly are a vital part of any garden. Bees are around the garden whenever it is warm enough, but butterflies tend to appear mainly in late summer. Bees not only supply a summery sound to the garden, they also provide honey and help with the pollination so essential to ensure seed for the next generation of plants. Although many garden plants supply them with nectar and pollen, bees and butterflies do have their favourites.

OREGANO (Origanum rotundifolium) *This attractive plant looks rather like a hop, with its green and reddish bracts, between which peep tiny, pink tubular flowers. All the origanums and marjorams are especially attractive to bees.*

COMMON LIME (Tillia x europaea) *These trees are too large for most gardens but as bees love their flowers perhaps one can be planted in a nearby hedge.*

SWEET SCABIOUS (Scabiosa caucasica) *Attractive not only to bees, this plant normally has lavender-blue flowers but there are some good cream and white varieties as well, and all have a sweet scent.*

BETONY (Stachys officinalis 'Rosea') *This is a rosy-pink form of the wild betony that grows in the hedgerows. It makes a good mid-border plant and attracts bees throughout the summer.*

MISS WILLMOTT'S GHOST (Eryngium giganteum) *A marvellous bee plant that acquired its common name after that lady's reputed habit of scattering its seed in her friends' gardens, leaving them to puzzle over the ensuing plants' provenance.*

BORAGE (Borago officinalis) *No bee garden should be without this splendid annual. Its starry blue flowers are pleasing and can be used to garnish food. The foliage is, of course, used as a herb. Once established, it will self-sow gently to provide late-summer colour.*

FENNEL (Foeniculum vulgare) *In flower this plant is always covered with bees. It is a very attractive plant but, if permitted, it seeds everywhere.*

BUTTERFLY BUSH (Buddleia davidii) *This bush is aptly named as it attracts butterflies as well as bees to its fragrant blossoms. Some of the darker, modern varieties have not got the same appeal as the more common forms.*

WHITE CLOVER (Trifolium repens) *Not many people would deliberately cultivate this weed in the garden but outside it, or in an odd patch of grass, it does prove an irresistible attraction to bees.*

HEBE (Hebe albicans) *This particular hebe is very attractive to bees, which smother its white flowers.*

Kent HONEY 1 LB. NET.

PERENNIALS

THE LEOPARD'S BANE, *Doronicum*, has the same cheerful yellow colouring that we associate with many daffodils and appears in the same season. Its daisy-like flowers fade less if grown in shade. This undemanding plant, which you forget out of season but always receive with a welcome on its return, is 2–3ft (60–90cm) tall, according to the variety that you grow. The only attention it needs is to be cut to the ground after flowering.

Bleeding heart, *Dicentra spectabilis*, is another old favourite of springtime, with its pink-and-white lockets hanging along the undersides of 2ft (60cm), arching stems. It likes moist soil and a bit of shade.

Of the many varieties of lungworts or pulmonarias, the earliest in general cultivation was soldiers and sailors, *Pulmonaria officinalis*, with its clusters of pink-and-blue flowers and spotted leaves – the more

PERENNIAL FAVOURITE Bleeding heart, Dicentra spectabilis, *is a perennial favourite in the cottage garden.*

SCENTED SELECTION Primroses, Primula vulgaris, *and some lungwort,* Pulmonaria officinalis, *nestle together.*

spots the better. Because the flowering season is early and the plain-leaved kinds tend to be lost in summer, lungworts with decorative leaves are often grown. *P. saccharata* 'Argentea', for example, whose silver sheen covers most of the leaf, is a popular variety for growing in shade in summer where it stands out and makes an admirable ground cover plant.

Lady's Mantle

Alchemilla mollis, the most widely grown lady's mantle today, is good ground cover. Native to the Caucasus, it was introduced to British gardens in 1874, but was never mentioned by William Robinson or Gertrude Jekyll and did not become well known or widely distributed until the 1950s. Its scalloped leaves glisten with raindrops after a shower, and its lime-green

CONTRASTING COLOURS Fiery spikes of orange-red montbretia, Crocosmia x crocosmiiflora, *and the bright green frothiness of lady's mantle,* Alchemilla mollis, *make effective partners. Typical cottage-garden perennials, they both have a tendency to spread.*

inflorescences are deliciously fresh in spring and early summer, although the plants need shearing back by late summer, so they can grow new leaves for the autumn. *A. mollis* is an incontinent self-seeder and its seedlings quickly take a firm hold. Often it puts itself in just the right place, somewhere that would be awkward to plant deliberately, such as under a garden seat or in a paving or wall crack. I do not go along with Margery Fish's permissiveness when she wrote "I never mind how many seedlings I find in the garden, for they are all welcome". You can have too much, even of a good thing.

Spurges

Spurges are charming traditional perennials. In spring the cypress spurge, *Euphorbia cyparissias*, throws up a mass of slender shoots that resemble young conifer seedlings, and it flowers then, too, producing green inflorescences. In autumn the leaves take on fine tints, especially when grown in sun, where it colonizes best, especially if outside the garden fence or on a rather hot bank.

The wood spurge, *Euphorbia amygdalloides*, has rosettes of dark, evergreen foliage on a low shrub, which are surmounted by a pale green inflorescence in spring and early summer. The best variety to grow is 'Rubra' ('Purpurea'), the foliage of which, especially at the young shoot tips, takes on a reddish-purple tinge in winter to add colour to that grey season. It makes an excellent companion for pale yellow primroses and the brighter yellow of an early dwarf daffodil such as *Narcissus* 'Tête-à-tête'.

Spring Flowers

I particularly associate spring in a cottage garden with the yellow fumitory, which has cheerful bunches of short, tubular spikes. This is *Corydalis lutea*, which loves the base of, or cracks in, a wall. Chimney bellflower, *Campanula pyramidalis*, with its long spikes of blue, sometimes white, saucer flowers in late summer also grows in walls. Traditionally grown as a biennial pot plant to stand in empty fireplaces, it is a remarkably persistent perennial and has a most endearing and unexpected presence.

Hardy auriculas are nothing like the fragile and easily damaged prize specimens reared by florist artisans in the last century, but, as easy-to-grow perennials taking their place with primroses and polyanthus, they are delightful plants and have their own special fragrance.

For me, late spring in seaside cottage gardens is always associated with huge mats of *Erigeron glaucus*, generally growing on a bank. This mauve daisy bears shortish rays when compared with its very large, green disc. A cheerful and obliging plant, evergreen and reasonably hardy even inland, it carries some flowers right through the summer. You seldom see it on sale, so I suppose it must pass from garden to garden, in the best "have-a-bit" tradition.

Early Summer Colour

Jacob's ladder, *Polemonium caeruleum*, with its ladder-like, pinnate leaves, is a 3ft (90cm) perennial, short-lived maybe but freely reproducing. The open, funnel-shaped flowers appear in early summer and are most often pale or deeper blue; the white form is pure in colour and pleasing.

Perennial cornflowers, *Centaurea montana*, are indestructible, every bit of damaged root ready to make a new plant. The species is mauve-blue with large, scented cornflowers on a 2ft (60cm) plant. It sprawls rather early in life, but if you cut it back it will grow

ORIENTAL POPPIES The perennial oriental poppies, Papaver orientale, are larger than their annual counterparts and tend to last longer.

PLEASING CHANGE Silver is not a common colour in the cottage garden, so lamb's ears, Stachys byzantina, makes a welcome exception.

WHITE AND YELLOW Libertia grandiflora and the day lily, Hemerocallis flava, mingle happily.

and flower again, although it may be rather prone to mildew the second time round. There is an albino and several other interesting colour selections, including pale blue and rosy mauve.

Gillenia trifoliata, once known as *Spiraea trifoliata*, is a real cottage-garden perennial, flowering in June. It was introduced to Britain from the United States in 1713. Three feet (90cm) tall, its elegant leaves, arranged in threes, are crowned by an insect-like cloud of hovering blossom, each flower bearing five narrow petals. As the stems and calyces are red, the contrast is the more marked.

Limonium latifolium, a perennial statice that covers itself with a mounded haze of tiny mauve flowers in late summer, is indestructible in a border with its

FETCHING DISPLAY Bellflowers, Campanula poscharskyana, *and a single and a double cultivar of the rock rose,* Helianthemum sp., *make a fetching display.*

PURPLE PAIR Irises and penstemons are unusual partners, but the contrast of shape and the subtle change of colour are particularly effective on this occasion.

deep tap roots – salt marshes are its natural habitat. The whole plant smells of carrion so, until you are aware of that, you may wonder where the dead bird or rat is lurking. The spikes of violet-blue flowers of the perennial *Salvia nemorosa* provide vivid colour in the border and its aromatic foliage might be more to your liking.

With *Armeria maritima*, the sea thrift, or sea pink as they call it in northern Britain, the whole plant forms a mound. The little globes of sweetly scented flowers open in early summer, and are typically mauve-pink, but there is tremendous variation from white to deep cherry-red. An untouched hummock will grow very big in a garden and may also contain an anthill. This has long been a favourite edging plant. Easily propagated, you can pull a plant to pieces and just stick bits into the border. Young plants treated in this way flower more freely than old.

Pansies & Campions

When I was young and before we substituted a deep bronzy thrift in the 1930s, we edged the beds in our rose garden with an old viola called 'Maggie Mott'; it is still available. At that time pansies, violas and violettas were florists' flowers for special cultivation in pots, but they have since taken their place in the garden. Many have been preserved, such as 'Irish Molly', which bears greenish blooms combined with a sort of off-brown, or 'Jackanapes', which has bright brown-and-yellow flowers.

I love the rose campion, *Lychnis coronaria*, which is a short-lived but self-sowing, summer-flowering perennial. Its basal bouquet of grey leaves is satisfying and its flowering stems, which branch stiffly – all arms and legs (like Meccano, as Margery Fish described it) – are a soothing background for the brilliant magenta moons. Such a flower colour is not to everyone's taste but it is certainly to mine. There are refined variants such as the pure white albino, *L.c.* 'Alba', and *L.c.* 'Occulata', which opens white but then develops a pale pink eye.

Golden Rod & Anemones

Associated with late summer are perennial sunflowers and coneflowers, *Rudbeckia*, golden rod, *Solidago vargaurea*, and, cooling down all this yellow, a drift of single white Japanese anemones, *Anemone hupehensis*. The pink Japanese anemones are good too, although the ring of yellow stamens at the flower's centre shows up less well than in the white of the species.

Cottage Favourites

*Perennial plants are the backbone of the cottage garden. They provide
the main source of colour and texture from spring through to the autumn.
Winter is their only dull time but even then there are a few to brighten
the grey months. Their arrival every year creates a framework against
which the temporary annuals and other plants can be used.*

KNOTWEED (Polygonum
affine) *A carpeting plant for
the front of the border, this
long-flowering plant turns
from pink to red.*

ROSE CAMPION (Lychnis coronaria)
*The grey, felted leaves contrast
well with the vivid cerise of the
blooms. There are quieter white forms.*

LADY'S MANTLE
(Alchemilla mollis) *Deadhead
the airy heads of green flowers
to prevent over-zealous
self-seeding.*

SNEEZEWEED (Helenium
'Moerheim Beauty') *This useful
late-season plant has
richly coloured,
daisy-like flowers.
A good plant for
cutting.*

SHASTA DAISY
(Leucanthemum maximum)
*This daisy has been popular
with generations of
gardeners. It is coarser than
other, what can loosely be
called, chrysanthemums.
In windy areas it
might need support.*

PENSTEMON
(Penstemon *'Drinkstone
Red'*) *Colourful plants
for midsummer,
these come in a range
of hues from purple to
light blue and, as here, red.*

TICKSEED
(Coreopsis verticillata)
*An attractive yellow
"daisy" that flowers
over a long period in summer, tickseed
is self-supporting, although the stems
and leaves look quite delicate.*

MULLEIN (Verbascum
olympicum) *The tall,
candelabra-like spikes are
densely packed with
yellow flowers and add
a statuesque quality to
a border. Many are
short-lived perennials
or biennials.*

BELLFLOWER (Campanula
lactiflora) *Large heads of lilac-
blue flowers supported by strong,
tall stems, bellflowers
are seen for a
long period
in summer.*

SAGE (Salvia nemorosa
'Superba') *The bright
annual sages can look
out of place in a cottage
garden, especially if
regimented, but there are
several less brash perennials
that are more at home.
Most vary from blue
to purple.*

The stamens are completed by a small green eye at the centre. These Japanese anemones hate being moved. Once established they are more than happy to take over, often extending their territory through the boundary fence to the roadside's verge.

Montbretia

The common montbretia, *Crocosmia* x *crocosmiiflora*, belongs to the late-summer cottage garden and, being invasive, you see it a great deal. Its orange colouring is rather brash on its own – kinder to the eye is another old montbretia, *C. pottsii*, which is small-flowered and warm red. *C. paniculata*, once known as *Antholyza* and corrupted to 'Aunt Eliza', is up to 5ft (150cm) tall with broad, ribbed, sword-shaped leaves and panicles of deep red flowers. Even when dead and brown, the leaves remain handsome. Its only requirements are well-drained soil and a place in the sun. It is particularly common in south-west Britain and throughout Ireland.

TRADITIONAL EDGING PLANTS Aubrieta and mossy saxifrage are ubiquitous cottage-garden plants. Both are low-growing and form large mats. They are therefore ideal for edging and spilling over a path, and aubrieta can also be planted in a wall. Shear it every year to keep it compact. Unless planted in moist soil, saxifrage does best if protected from the hot, midday sun.

MAINSTAY OF THE COTTAGE GARDEN Lupins are one of the traditional mainstays of the cottage garden, valued for their strong, vivid spikes of white, yellow, pink, red and purple, which rise majestically in early summer. They are short-lived, however, and are best raised from seed each year. Plant them in their flowering position in the autumn.

A Typical Cottage Garden

Just before writing this, a friend sent me a birthday card, a photograph by Kenneth Scowen depicting a cottage and its flower-lined garden path in spring. The path was of crazy paving, which has become fashionable only in the last sixty years; although I recognize its usefulness, I have always disliked its fussiness. The detail in any traditional cottage garden should be very much concentrated in the plants. To

me, man-made features, such as a bird table with mini-thatched roofing, are in danger of bordering on the twee. As for plaster or plastic gnomes, bunnies, pelicans, flamingos and the rest, they give me the creeps. Each to his own, but in my opinion it can hardly be disputed that they detract from, rather than set off, the garden plants.

In the birthday-card photograph I noted several ingredients that are typical of the cottage garden but which I have not yet mentioned. There was the mossy saxifrage, *Saxifraga hypnoides*, whose soft green cushions are mantled with pink, red or white blossom, each chalice-shaped flower looking proudly upwards to the sky. In my garden the sparrows inexplicably took to ripping the blossom to pieces, but sparrows are funny birds, behaving quite differently from garden to garden or, indeed, from one year to another. If you give up a plant for a few years, a new generation of sparrows will arise that will not know it and so may leave it alone.

Then there was yellow alyssum – not the annual sweet alyssum – but the bright mustard-yellow, long-lived perennial, *Alyssum saxatile*. This old favourite has great vitality but its colour is considered crude in refined circles, in which case the pale yellow variety, *A.s.* 'Citrinus' (alias *A.s.* 'Silver Queen'), is a good substitute, although less robust.

There is nothing wrong with the mustard-yellow colouring of the alyssum species but it does appear crude when alternated with one of the bright purple aubrietas and the magenta-carmine rock phlox, *Phlox subulata* 'Temiskaming'. These are excellent plants in their own way and a single juxtaposition of the alyssum with the aubrieta could be most effective, whereas, when hammered in with repetition, nausea quickly sets in. The rock phloxes are wonderful, cushion-forming plants, appearing a little later than the mainstream of aubrietas. *P.s.* 'Temiskaming' has been introduced only since the Second World War, but the softer pinks and mauves have been cultivated in Britain for many years. The vigorous, pale blue *P.s.* 'G.F. Wilson' is one of my favourites. (Wilson himself gave his property to the Royal Horticultural Society where its famous Wisley garden is now located and open to the public).

Many of the tighter, cushion-forming phloxes are grouped under the banner (as Will Ingwersen phrased it) of *Phlox douglasii*. That species seems not to exist, although perhaps, like the Cheshire Cat's grin, it once did and you cannot be certain it will not re-materialize. If, as *P. douglasii*, you find yourself with a prettily rounded, pale mauve flower with dark spots at the base of the petals, looking like the design for a cotton print frock, you have a good plant. I combined it with common thyme, the small shrub that also flowers in late spring and is exactly the same colour. The two looked absolutely charming together until the day when a paying visitor came and swiped the phlox. I have not seen once since.

Tulips

Tulips also featured in my cottage-garden birthday card, scattered among other plants. This is a happy treatment if you are not constantly moving plants around. Undisturbed tulips, especially on a stiffish soil, will continue in good health indefinitely. I have clumps that have not diminished in thirty years. The size of flower will not be prize winning, but then the largest tulips tend to look out of scale in a cottage-garden context anyway.

I warned, when writing of Madonna lilies on page 33, that broken, virus-infected tulips could weaken lilies with the same disease to the point of extinction. But if you would rather have the tulips than the lilies, good luck to you. The beautiful streaky kinds have a long, popular history and feature in all the old Dutch flower paintings. The fashion reached Britain from Flanders. Broken tulips are less popular than they were, but the cottage garden remains a stronghold. Tulip foliage dies off far less obtrusively than that of the daffodil; tulips are, in many ways, to be preferred, if you do not want your garden to be a scene of dereliction by late spring.

COTTAGE CLASSICS Sweet-smelling wallflowers and ever-cheerful tulips have stood the test of time as cottage-garden favourites. Every garden should have them.

Autumn Flowers

*Colour can last well into the autumn with a little planning,
giving interest to the garden for an extended period.*

❖ *JAPANESE ANEMONE* (Anemone *x*
hybrida *'Honorine Joubert')* These
nodding, slightly cupped flowers are
available in white and pink. Prefers partial
shade and well-drained soil.

❖ *ICE PLANT* (Sedum spectabile
'Brilliant') Flat heads of dense, rose-pink
flowers have great appeal for butterflies
above fleshy, grey-green leaves. Prefers full
sun and well-drained soil.

❖ *GOLDEN ROD* (Solidago
'Goldenmosa') An old-fashioned, clump-
forming perennial that has sprays of tufted,
mimosa-like, yellow flower heads. Prefers
full sun and well-drained soil.

❖ *CHRYSANTHEMUM* (Chrysanthem-
um *'Brietner')* This variety is fully double
but there are many different flower forms
that come in a range of colours. Prefers full
sun and well-drained soil.

❖ *CONEFLOWER* (Rudbeckia
fulgida *'Goldstrum')* Prominent, conical,
black centres differentiate this plant from
others with daisy-like flowers. Prefers full
sun and moist soil.

❖ *MICHELMAS DAISY* (Aster novae-
angliae *'Herbstschnee')* A compact
perennial with fringed, daisy-like white
petals and a yellow centre. Prefers full
sun and well-drained soil.

TRADITIONAL SHRUBS

ONE OF MY EARLIEST MEMORIES in my own village is of a small, cottage front garden with a hedge of the cheerful, red-flowered Japanese quince on the right side of the path. As the path was short so was the hedge, which was clipped several times a year but not prevented from flowering on that account. The cottage itself was later named Japonica – the rather misleading name widely given to this shrub. Japonica simply means Japanese and is applied to many other plants too. We used to know this red-flowered quince as *Pyrus japonica*, but its name has since gone through many vicissitudes, being currently *Chaenomeles speciosa*. It can be, and often is, trained against a wall and does not object to a shady aspect.

Jew's mallow, *Kerria japonica*, is a most persistent, suckering shrub with green, cane-like young shoots. Although perfectly hardy, it is generally planted against a wall or fence, to which its long shoots can be tied. The tallest and most popular variety of this is the double-flowered *K.j.* 'Pleniflora' – its bright yellow pompons full of petals appear in late spring. If correctly pruned, with old, flowered wood re-moved annually, it is a handsome, 8–10ft- (240–300cm-) high shrub that enjoys a shady position, as the flowers have a tendency to bleach in the sun. In practice, this variety is seldom pruned at all and looks cheerfully scruffy in many gardens. The single-flowered species grows less tall and is far more elegant, looking good with an underplanting of yellow and white polyanthus.

Currants & Cotoneasters

The ubiquitous flowering currant, *Ribes sanguineum*, whose flowers smell of tom cats, must have become popular soon after its introduction to Britain from North America in 1826. In their early spring season, the pink flowers are often combined with yellow forsythia – uncomfortable bedfellows, especially in hedging where the two are usually alternated and grow stiffly, following their annual pruning. Flowering currant is easily forced indoors, where its delicate flowers open almost pure white.

Cotoneaster horizontalis is the best of its genus for cottage gardens, either bracketing from the top of a retaining wall or plastering itself, without assistance,

LONG-BLOSSOMING SHRUB Lavatera thuringiaca *forms a large shrub with a long succession of papery, pink flowers.*

COMPANIONABLE CLIMBER Clematis *blends well with many other plants. Here one is peeping out from under the delicate flowers of* Gillenia trifoliata.

layer upon layer against a wall or fence. A shady aspect suits it as well as any; in fact, it is quite happy wherever it finds itself. The close-textured fishbone structure of its branches is very positive. It leafs in early spring and the foliage turns deep crimson in late autumn before dropping. During autumn, also, this crimson colouring is combined with the pure red of its massive crop of berries, which will remain until spring unless eaten by the birds, which is very likely as they devour the fruit in many gardens. This plant is an all-rounder; if despised, this is only because it is so obliging and easy to grow.

Seaside Shrubs

Big bushes of red and purple fuchsias, *Fuchsia magellanica* 'Riccartonii', are especially prevalent near the sea where they grow much bigger than inland as they do not die back so much in the winter. They withstand any amount of pruning both by humans and by the weather, but do need tidying up in the spring.

The most common seaside shrub must be tamarisk, *Tamarix pentandra*, with its distinctive foliage and feathery plumes of tiny pink flowers. Other predominantly seaside shrubs, although also grown inland, are the escallonias and evergreen euonymus. The larger-leaved escallonias are an especially good defence against salt winds, notably *Escallonia macrantha*, with its reddish-pink flowers. *Euonymus japonicus* is grown as evergreen hedging in the front line against the elements. Its oval leaves are highly polished, so they never look dull and dirty. There are many yellow-leaved and variegated forms – all good in their way. I would stand up for this despised shrub and suggest that a few specimens, allowed to grow fairly freely, look better than a depersonalized, clipped hedge.

Cottage Favourites

Shrubs have not been a major feature in cottage gardens, although cottagers have always used them to decorate walls. Those that appear elsewhere have to earn their keep by being particularly attractive or fragrant, or by bearing fruit. Nowadays everybody is more shrub-conscious and there are a great number that fit happily into the cottage scene.

FUCHSIA (Fuchsia magellanica) *This hardy fuchsia has long been a cottage-garden favourite. In warmer areas it makes a decorative hedge.*

HYDRANGEA (Hydrangea macrophylla) *Few gardens are without a form of hydrangea. They come in a wide range of colours, which to an extent depends on the soil conditions in the garden.*

CLEMATIS (Clematis x jackmanii) *An excellent climber for walls or trellises or to thread through other plants, this clematis is a prolific bloomer in mid-summer.*

WISTERIA
(Wisteria sinensis)
*Normally associated with
large houses, wisteria clothes
the fronts of many cottages.
Masses of pendulous heads
of blue flowers appear
during the early summer,
with occasional blooms
in late summer.*

SHRUB ROSE
(Rosa rugosa *'Alba'*)
*These make wonderful
shrubs with red, pink or white
flowers and interesting hips.
The white form is good for
brightening a dark corner.*

TAMARISK (Tamarix
pentandra) *A light, airy
shrub with feathery leaves
and flowers, tamarisk is
particularly happy
near the sea.*

TREE MALLOW
(Lavatera thuringiaca)
*A very old garden plant, tree
mallow has become particularly
popular of late. The tall, shrubby
bush produces masses of pink
flowers over a very long
season, from early
summer to late autumn.
It suits the cottage setting
admirably.*

*FLORIBUNDA
ROSE* (Rosa *'Florence
Mary Morse'*) *Red roses
have always been one of
the most popular with
generations of gardeners.
In Victorian times they came to
symbolize "love" and today
they are one of the few flowers
that retain their
meaning.*

TRADITIONAL HERBS

Herbs have been in cultivation since ancient times; they may even have been the reason for the development of the cottage garden. Whereas vegetables were grown in communal strips or fields, herbs were planted in odd spots close to the house. This random planting later became interspersed with decorative flowers and shrubs and the cottage garden came into existence. Herbs had three main uses: medicinal, culinary and odorous.

Herbs to Cure

Nowadays herbs are rarely grown in our gardens for medicinal purposes, although there are many books that advocate their use as alternatives to modern medicines. The only successful medicinal use of herbs that I have come across is for the removal of warts: treat them with juice from the stems of greater celandine, *Chelidonium majus*. This celandine grows wild and is often found close to a cottage in the verge or hedge near the front gate. The pretty, double form of this species makes a good cottage plant and it is for this, rather than its medicinal properties, that I would recommend it for growing in the garden.

Herbs to Flavour

The main reason for including herbs in our gardens is to use them for flavouring food. In the past, herbs provided a good alternative to the expensive spices used by the rich. Their taste disguised the blandness of a cottager's food or the fact that it was not always fresh. Today they are included in all types of dishes to add a variety of subtle flavours. But unfortunately it is all too convenient to snatch a pinch of herbs from a packet or jar rather than to grow and harvest them fresh from our own gardens. Although more herbs are available to the cottager now than ever before, fewer are grown than in earlier times for practical purposes and only half a dozen or so are used on a regular basis.

Herbs to Scent

Within the house, herbs are still valued for their fragrance, although one of their original uses – overcoming the smell of dampness and other malodours – is rarely relevant. Few people now strew their floors or stuff their mattresses with sweet-smelling herbs, and they are mainly appreciated today for the pleasure they give when displayed either as cut flowers or as dried material in preparations such as pot-pourri. Either way, they bring a wonderful scent into the house and provide some attractive decorations.

VARIED HERB Sage, an invaluable herb in the kitchen, is available in several different colours. In front of this golden sage, Salvia officinalis *'Icterina', grows the dark form of the equally useful oregano,* Origanum vulgare.

EXERCISING RESTRAINT Most herbs can be grown easily in the open ground but there are some, such as this mint, Mentha spicata, *that, because of their wandering habit, are best confined so they cannot choke other herbs.*

THE HERB GARDEN

THE HERB GARDEN IS AN EMOTIVE SUBJECT. Many people fall in love with the concept of creating one but find that in practice it is difficult and time-consuming work and that the result may be disappointing. The cottage garden did not generally have a separate herb section; instead the individual herbs were mixed in with other plants. For convenience, many of them were grown within easy reach of the kitchen door so that fresh herbs could be added to the pot while cooking.

Common Perennial Herbs

One of the herbs most often seen at the kitchen door is mint. Several different types can be grown (including apple mint, ginger mint, peppermint, pineapple mint and lemon mint), all of which are worth exploring. Spearmint, *Mentha spicata*, is the most popular. Used as a culinary herb for flavouring food and for adding a refreshing taste to drinks, it is easy to grow – perhaps too easy. The plant spreads rapidly, running underground to form a large mat. The traditional way to control it is to sink an old, bottomless bucket into the ground and plant the mint within its confining walls. In late summer and autumn it produces spikes of pale mauve flowers which attract bees. You may dry the leaves for use in winter when the herb dies back.

Traditionally during spring, before the new crop of onions was ready, chives, *Allium schoenoprasum*, provided a substitute flavouring. Their decorative, rounded heads of purplish flowers are best displayed when the herb is grown beside a path.

Sweet marjoram, *Origanum marjoram*, is easy to grow and has a place in any sunny border. Finely chopped, the leaves are excellent when added to salads and fish dishes. They have a spicy, aromatic scent, although this is not as strong as that of oregano, *O. vulgare*, which is commonly used in Mediterranean cooking. The stems and root-stalks of both are also edible and good in salads. The pink flowers attract bees and butterflies.

Fennel, *Foeniculum vulgare*, adds a statuesque quality to any planting and is most attractive, with finely cut leaves borne on tall stems. The whole plant can be used in a variety of ways, raw and cooked, and adds a pronounced aniseed flavour. Be sure to gather all the seeds as fennel self-sows vigorously and, once established, the seedlings are not easy to pull out.

Annual & Biennial Herbs

The commonest of the annual herbs must surely be parsley, *Petroselimun crispum*. Several different varieties are available – all are rich sources of vitamins and minerals quite apart from making attractive garnishings for almost any dish. To hasten germination, leave the seeds to soak overnight before planting and keep the seed trays in a warm place until the seed has germinated.

Basil, *Ocimum basilicum*, is another popular annual herb and the leaves, with their sweet, slightly spicy flavour, are excellent sprinkled in salads; it is particularly good served with tomato salad and added to pasta dishes. Slugs seem especially partial to this herb so it is best grown on a windowsill in pots.

Dill, *Anethum graveolens*, was used extensively both for its culinary and medicinal qualities. The leaves add a distinctive flavour to boiled new potatoes and can be used as a garnish. The seeds are commonly added to pickles, breads and cakes. It produces copious quantities of seed and is easy to cultivate but should not be grown together with fennel as the two may cross-pollinate.

Another widely grown herb that has been cultivated since ancient times is angelica, *Angelica archangelica*. Like dill, it is a member of the cow parsley family and bears large heads of small flowers radiating from the top of each stem. Angelica is best known today as a culinary decoration, for which purpose the stems are crystallized. The leaves may be cooked with fruits to reduce their acidity.

Mustard, *Brassica nigra*, is rarely grown now in cottage gardens, although it has been in cultivation since prehistoric times as a medicinal and a culinary herb. Its bright yellow flowers are often seen in swathes across the fields, where it is grown as a green manure crop. Its leaves, stems, flowers and seeds all have culinary uses and the plant may easily be grown in a cottage garden.

Herbs as Shrubs

As well as the many annual and herbaceous perennial herbs, there are several shrubby species. Three of these are essential to every cottage garden: sage, rosemary and lavender. Not only are they useful but their very appearance adds a traditional look.

Sage, *Salvia officinalis*, is one of the most important herbs in the kitchen. The leaves should be picked in summer, just before the flowers open, and used fresh or dried. As well as the common green-leaved form, there are others with variegated or purple leaves. The flowers are generally violet in colour and attract bees. Sages prefer a sunny, well-drained position.

Rosemary, *Rosmarinus officinalis*, is indispensable. Although it was put to many uses in the past, it is now mainly a herb for the kitchen. The needle-like leaves may be crumbled when dried or chopped fresh and added to meat dishes, particularly lamb. The

DECORATIVE HERB Chives, Allium schoenoprasum, *are useful herbs that can be grown either in the flower borders or, as here, with lettuce in the vegetable garden. In either location they lend a delicate charm.*

flowers, which may also be used in salad dishes, are generally light blue, but some are darker blue or purple. There are also white- and pink-flowered forms, although these are not so attractive in my opinion. Plant in a warm, well-drained position out of the way of cold winds.

It is impossible to imagine a cottage garden without lavender, *Lavandula angustifolia*, with its summery haze of mauve-blue flowers rising above soft grey foliage. The medicinal properties of this plant are still valued today and its essential oil is a common ingredient of many cosmetic preparations. Both the flowers and leaves of this shrub have a strong but fresh, clean fragrance. In cottage gardens, lavender may occasionally be seen edging a flower border, holding back the profusion of plants normally allowed to sprawl on to the path.

Cottage Favourites

The first gardens were probably entirely devoted to herbs, both for medicinal and culinary uses. Nowadays very few people grow them for curing ailments, but many are still grown for use in cooking or for perfuming the house. For convenience they are often grown near the kitchen door. In this position, the cook can quickly take what is needed. Most can be dried for use in winter.

ROSEMARY (Rosmarinus officinalis) *A wonderful aromatic shrub, rosemary can be used for flavouring meat dishes or for adding fragrance to pot-pourri.*

CHIVES (Allium schoenoprasum) *Perennial bulbs, chives are a member of the onion family. They are used raw in a number of dishes, particularly salads.*

BASIL (Ocimum basilicum) *Grown from seed, the leaves from this annual can be used in cooked dishes or added to salads, particularly tomatoes. There is also an attractive, purple-leaved variety.*

PARSLEY (Petroselinum crispum) *Grown annually from seed, parsley is one of those indispensable herbs used for garnishing as well as in cooking.*

THYME (Thymus vulgaris) *The fragrant leaves of the low, carpeting thymes have extensive uses in cooking. A very popular plant with the bees.*

BAY (Laurus nobilis) *This herb has been used in cooking for generations. It is used as a flavouring and is rarely eaten itself.*

SAGE (Salvia officinalis)
*A shrub, sage is another
great cooking favourite.
It comes in several
different forms.*

LOVAGE
(Levisticum
officinale) *Not such
a frequently seen herb,
lovage is a perennial
with a distinctive,
strong flavour.*

MINT (Mentha spicata)
*There are many different varieties
of this popular herb to
sample in drinks and
a wide variety
of dishes.*

FENNEL
(Foeniculum vulgare)
*An attractive perennial,
all parts of fennel, including
roots, can be used in cooking.*

FRUIT & VEGETABLES

N THE PAST, COTTAGERS either had to grow their own fruit and vegetables or go without. They did not have the money to buy them even when they were available locally. Home produce was also a source of income, as it could be sold at local markets. I can remember my great uncle setting off for the market with fruit and vegetables. He also sold lettuces and other vegetables from the gate in front of his cottage.

FORCED RHUBARB A common site in a cottage garden is that of rhubarb being forced, using old buckets. Here, however, the cottager seems to have forgotten the buckets and has left them on a little longer than he should have.

YOUNG VEGETABLE GARDEN In early spring this vegetable garden still shows a lot of bare earth. The early peas and broad beans are doing well and the spring cabbages, planted the previous autumn, have reached maturity.

Today it is no longer a matter of going without, but it is nevertheless well worth growing one's own fruit and vegetables. Despite the amount of time spent tending them, which if costed out would make them more expensive than those from local supermarkets, growing your own is very rewarding. Cost has little to do with it anyway.

Growing for Taste & Convenience

Fresh produce always tastes infinitely better than that bought in a shop. This is partly because it has just been picked but also because the varieties available to gardeners are usually more flavoursome than those offered in shops. Commercially grown fruit and vegetables are often bred for their ability to keep their colour, to travel without bruising and for other practical qualities, rather than for their taste. With the exception of apples and potatoes, the name of the variety of a fruit or vegetable is rarely given. Yet you can ask any vegetable gardener and he will be able to reel off proudly the names of all the different varieties he grows. Whereas seed merchants know that taste is one of the main reasons for choosing a particular variety, greengrocers often think it is only appearance that sells their wares.

Taste is not the only reason for growing your own fruit and vegetables; convenience and choice are others. Convenience because they are just outside the back door and you do not have to trek to the shops to get them, and choice because a well-stocked garden presents you with a wide range of produce – you can select whatever you like, even out of season if you freeze the surplus.

Exercise & Fresh Air

Having sung the praises of growing vegetables, it has to be admitted that it is time-consuming and, sometimes, strenuous work. But it is also very relaxing – providing exercise and fresh air and helping to relieve the stresses and strains of a hectic working life. There is something extremely satisfying and attractive about a well-organized vegetable garden and, of course, the pleasures to be had from consuming the fruits of one's labour or giving produce to friends cannot be over-estimated.

THE FRUIT GARDEN

FRUIT AND NUTS HAVE ALWAYS been part of the countryman's diet and a cottage garden would not seem complete without a few fruit trees and bushes. Some, such as blackberries and hazelnuts, could be had for free from the hedgerows, while others, such as damsons and bullace, were planted as hedgerow specimens, where they took up no space in the garden and yet provided a generous crop.

Fruit Trees

Most cottage gardens had apple trees both for dessert and cooking apples. These were the standard trees that grew to full height rather than the stunted ones you see today grown on dwarfing stock. If you have room, use standards as they give character to the garden and provide a wonderful dappled shade in the summer. There is a vast range of types available, including many of the older varieties. This is also true of pears, plums and cherries. In days gone by, several acres of sweet cherries needed to be planted to overcome the problem of bird predation, but with modern netting facilities it is now possible to grow them in a small garden. Morello cherries are useful as they can be planted against shady walls.

Fruit Bushes

All three forms of currants have always been popular: red, black and white. Blackcurrants are especially tasty, making wonderful jam, and redcurrant jelly is a delicious accompaniment to meat. White currants are the least popular but they can still be found and are well worth growing for variety.

Canes & Perennial Fruit

Raspberries and strawberries, although now widely available from "pick-your-own" farms, are best from one's own garden. Many of the old cottagers would be amazed at how the season for these two fruits has been extended in recent years. Both are excellent when fresh but are also used extensively in jams and may be bottled and even frozen.

ALL-TIME FAVOURITES Strawberries really need no introduction. They are easy to grow and are one of the most luscious fruits produced in the cottage garden.

COOKING APPLES No cottage garden is complete without at least one apple tree for cooking apples.

JUST READY FOR EATING Fruit trees of all kinds appear in the cottage garden. Juicy pears are favourites.

Gooseberries have always enjoyed popularity in spite of their vicious spines. One of their main drawbacks was their susceptibility to mildew, but there are now resistant varieties. For many years, the gooseberry has been one of the show fruits, with gardeners vying with each other to produce the largest berry. Traditionally they are served with mackerel, their acidity balancing the richness of the fish.

Rhubarb, a perennial, was grown widely, originally for medicinal purposes, but later as a fruit and for tarts. It also makes a superb wine and chutney. Rhubarb needs little attention once planted except for an annual mulch of manure or compost.

A number of fruits have now all but disappeared. Of medlars, bullace, chequers and quinces, only the quince is still occasionally seen. It adds a distinctive flavour to apple dishes, makes a delicious jelly and can also be used to make chutney.

Cottage Favourites

Soft fruits are so tasty, attractive and versatile that no cottage garden should be without at least two or three different sorts. There can be few people who have not experienced the pleasure of picking a fresh strawberry or raspberry and putting it straight into their mouth on a warm summer's day. In the winter, soft fruits that have been bottled or made into jams can be a good source of vitamins and, of course, provide a welcome variation to the winter diet.

CHERRIES (Prunus *hybs.*) *Birds love cherries. To avoid losing all your crop to them, grow the tree against a wall and cover with a net when the fruit is forming.*

REDCURRANTS (Ribes sativum) *Wonderful eaten raw with a sprinkling of sugar, redcurrants also make a good jelly for toast or with roasts.*

RASPBERRIES (Rubus idaeus) *Do not wash raspberries that are to be eaten raw as it will spoil their flavour. Do, however, make a careful check for worms or bad spots.*

GOOSEBERRIES (Ribes grossularia) *Gooseberries are good for cooking and bottling and are a valuable source of vitamins in winter. Try them fresh with sugar and cream.*

LOGANBERRIES (Rubus *x* loganobaccus) *Choose a sheltered site for loganberries as the canes can be damaged or killed by severe frosts.*

WILD STRAWBERRIES (Fragaria vesca) *These have a superb flavour and are the best strawberries for jam.*

BLUEBERRIES (Vaccinium *sp.*) *Blueberries are useful for growing in colder regions where other soft fruits do not thrive. Although laborious to harvest, their unusual taste makes the effort worthwhile.*

GARDEN STRAWBERRIES (Fragaria *x* ananassa) *Although tending to lack the flavour of wild strawberries, garden strawberries produce a bigger crop. Nowadays, there are many different varieties which, if all are grown, can provide a continuous supply of fruit all summer.*

THE VEGETABLE GARDEN

MEAT WAS GENERALLY in somewhat short supply for the cottager, so vegetables, by necessity, formed the basis of his meals. Consequently vegetables had priority over fruit in the cottage garden, despite being more demanding of time and space.

WINTER'S DAY Purple sprouting, a hardy brassica, will survive wintry conditions and towards the end of the season will provide a succession of succulent flower heads for cooking over several weeks.

STAPLE CROP Potatoes are one of the staple vegetables of the cottager's diet. Here is a crop in mid-season.

The Potato

It is often assumed that the mainstay of traditional vegetable gardens was the potato. This was not always so, particularly in the south, where for a long while potatoes were not an accepted part of the diet. Nowadays their popularity is again on the decline. This is partly because they are cheap to buy at the farm gate, but also because they take up so much space, both when they are in the ground and when in storage. In addition, not as many are eaten. However, even though there may be room only for a couple of rows of earlies, a few roots must be grown as the taste of the first potatoes out of the soil is one of the highlights of the year. My parents always used to celebrate the first to be dug each year by eating a meal composed entirely of potatoes. They are a good crop to plant in a new or reclaimed garden as they are useful for helping to clear the ground.

When choosing varieties from among the many available, don't restrict yourself to old ones – the most important criteria are flavour and texture. Buy small quantities of several varieties and find which you like best both for flavour and for texture.

Root Vegetables

Country people have always been keen on root crops, unlike many of their town relatives, who tended to look down on them as cattle feed. Having been born and lived most of my life in the country, I am passionately fond of many root vegetables. Parsnips are undoubtedly one of my favourites. They need a deep, stone-free soil that has been manured the previous season (as, indeed, do most of the root vegetables). Although one of the earliest to be sown, parsnips are among the latest to crop; many say they should not be harvested until after the first frosts, which sweeten the flavour, but I am not certain whether this is really true.

Carrots are another popular root crop. They are one of the earliest vegetables to mature in the garden and, as with potatoes, the flavour of the first pickings is something to be relished. They can be stored in dry sand or peat over winter but many country people simply leave them in the ground until they need them, although this may mean putting up with the inconvenience of a few slug holes.

Beetroot has been in cultivation since Roman times. Originally it was grown not for its root but for its leaves, which were used instead of spinach.

The globe varieties now commonly grown are a relatively recent development, replacing the long-rooted forms. The root is delicious eaten hot as a winter vegetable and, of course, cooked and chilled as an accompaniment for salad.

Turnips and swedes are in fact members of the cabbage family, although, unlike most cabbages, they have a swollen root system. In the past they were the staple diet of country people, both as vegetables in their own right and as a chief ingredient of stews.

VIGOROUS SWISS CHARD Sometimes know as seakale beet, Swiss chard is a member of the beetroot family. Its leaves are cooked and eaten like spinach.

WELL-ORDERED VEGETABLE PATCH Vegetables are arranged in their rows with bean poles in evidence and young vegetables are protected with wire netting.

The young tops of the turnip may be cooked as greens. Unfortunately they are not so popular these days but they still make a very tasty vegetable and it is certainly worth growing a row or two. Kohlrabi is often thought of as a root vegetable but it is in fact a cross between the turnip and the cabbage, with a swollen stem that, when cooked, has its own distinct flavour. The stems should be picked when they are the size of a tennis ball, otherwise they become very hard and woody. Many people assume that kohlrabi is a modern vegetable but cottagers have been growing it for over a century.

Peas & Beans

Peas and beans have also always been a staple of the countryman's diet. The sight of rows of runner beans climbing their poles with bright red flowers peeking out from the leaves, or peas scrambling up their

twiggy sticks is certainly one that is associated with a cottage garden. A reason for their continued popularity is that instead of eating them all you can set aside some to dry as seed for the following year's crop. This way you do not need to take up valuable ground space for another year while the plants run to seed (which is the case with other vegetables except potatoes). Many gardeners still save their own seed from favourite varieties, allowing a few pods to ripen and collecting the seed from them when it becomes dry. If you do this, make certain that your original crop is not an F1 hybrid as, if it is, it will not come true the following year but will revert to one of the original parents.

Both peas and beans are now available in dwarf, non-climbing forms as well as in the traditional, high-growing types which need support. An advantage of short forms is that they do not take up so much space and in theory require little support, although peas are helped with short sticks or supporting strings tied along each side. The hitherto low-growing French beans can now be purchased in a climbing version. The taller varieties have the advantage that they produce a larger crop but, unless you are freezing them, there is a limit to the number you will require at any one time. It is often better to sow several rows, over the course of the spring, that will provide a continuing supply rather than one large row that will crop all at once. Again there are so many varieties to choose from that the only way of selecting is to try several and see which one suits your own palate.

The Cabbage Family

The cabbage family (brassicas) provides many basic vegetables for the cottage garden: brussel sprouts, winter and spring cabbage, broccoli, purple-sprouting calabrese, cauliflower, various forms of kale – the list seems endless. Cabbage is not as popular as it once was – too many memories of school cooking have spoilt its reputation – but steamed, rather than boiled to death, it can be an extremely flavoursome vegetable. The advantage of the brassicas, and cabbage in particular, is that with careful planning there can be some ready to eat throughout the year, unlike most of the other vegetables that have a very short season. Even brussels, which once had a relatively limited season, can now be cropped from autumn through to early spring if you grow several varieties.

If space is limited, it is perhaps best to concentrate on those brassicas that provide a repeat picking, such as brussels or sprouting broccoli, rather than those that produce just one head, such as cauliflowers. But if you have plenty of room grow a whole range and it will provide an enjoyable and diverse diet. Brassicas should be planted in well-firmed soil that is rich in organic material – digging in any left-overs from the previous crop will improve it greatly.

The Onion Family

Leeks are another cottage-garden favourite, not only for eating but also for showing. For eating, they can be planted in any fertile soil, preferably in a shallow trench that is filled as the leeks grow, to encourage long, blanched stems. For showing purposes there are all sorts of tricks, not part of our domain, used to produce prize specimens. Related to the leek is, of course, the onion – another basic of the countryman's diet. Modern varieties of leeks will over-winter well and may be left in the ground until they are required; onions need to be lifted and dried in the early autumn but may then be stored throughout the winter. Bulbous onions are generally grown from sets (small onions from the previous year) but spring onions are raised from seed.

Salad Vegetables

Spring onions, of course, are used mainly in salads. I find it amazing that country people bothered with salads as they always seem too "lightweight" to fill the country stomach, which was used to a heavy diet of root crops. But even from quite early times the cottage gardener has grown lettuce, radish, cucumber and, more recently, tomatoes. Cucumbers and tomatoes would have been grown out-of-doors, often on the top of an old compost heap, on a pile of manure or on a raised ridge of earth (hence the name ridge cucumbers). But during the last century, surprisingly, many cottagers quickly accepted the idea of the greenhouse, using it to raise seedlings and vegetables such as tomatoes.

A HARVEST TO BE PROUD OF The most rewarding part of growing vegetables is harvesting them. It is incredibly satisfying pulling from the ground vegetables you sowed as seed in the spring.

Marrows & Spinach

Marrows were possibly the most widely cultivated of the cottage vegetables. Easy to grow, rich in vitamins and suitable for a host of culinary uses (as a vegetable, for baking and stuffing and to make jams, pickles and chutneys), they could be found in almost every garden, even in towns. They provide excellent camouflage for an old compost heap as they grow on rich, moisture-retentive soil. To store them, hang the marrows in a string bag in a frost-free place for use in winter. Young marrows (courgettes) have a more delicate and sweeter flavour.

There are various kinds of spinach. True spinach may be the most difficult to grow (needing rich soil and disliking both hot, dry weather and cold, wet conditions), but the pleasures derived from eating spinach picked fresh from the garden more than compensate for any extra care you may need to take. Spinach beet (perpetual spinach) is easier to grow as it is more tolerant of the weather and poor soil and provides a constant crop, but the leaves are coarser and the flavour less subtle.

COLOURFUL RESIDENT OF THE VEGETABLE PATCH The size and shape of pumpkins make them appealing to children, but bear in mind that they take up a lot of space.

VEGETABLES WITH CHARACTER With their idiosyncratic shapes, squashes appeal to many gardeners for the character and colour that they add to the vegetable patch. Grow them in a soil rich in organic matter.

Cottage Favourites

No cottage garden is complete without a vegetable patch. The lush green of vegetables complements the cottage-garden flowers and the neat, straight rows they make add some order to the riot of colour. Of course, the principle reason for growing vegetables is to put food on the table but you should not underestimate the sheer pleasure that raising them also provides.

HORSERADISH (Armoracia rusticana)
Horseradish is not so frequently grown nowadays but there is nothing like fresh horseradish sauce. Plant pieces of root in the spring and dig up the plant in the autumn.

LEEKS (Allium porrum) *A valuable crop that overwinters in the ground, sow leeks in the spring and plant out in early summer. They are delicious in stews and soups.*

POTATOES (Solanum tuberosum) *Potatoes were one of the cottager's mainstays. New potatoes fresh from the garden are particularly delicious.*

RADISHES (Raphaanus sativus) *Quick and easy to grow, use radishes as a catch crop between other, slower-growing vegetables.*

PARSNIPS
(Pastinaca sativa)
*These are a favourite
root crop for the winter,
which you can keep in
the ground until required.
Sow in early spring.*

CARROTS
(Daucus
carota sativus)
*If you sow carrots
throughout the spring
and early summer, you
will have a succession
of crops. Sow them
sparsely to avoid having to
thin them out. Store over
winter in dry sand or peat.*

BEETROOT
(Beta vulgaris)
*Beetroot is excellent for
salads and pickling.
Sow successionally
in spring and
take care not to bruise
or tear the skin when
harvesting or the colour
will bleed during cooking.*

TWO

COTTAGE-GARDEN FEATURES

The cottage garden is not the place for startling, attention-grabbing features. The essence of the cottage garden is informality,  and traditional cottage-garden features reinforce this image, tending to be of a subdued, humble, essentially rustic nature. In fact, you may not think of cottage-garden features as features at all, as most of them are so simple or so much a part of the garden that they are taken for granted. Many, such as pathways and hedges, are an essential part of the garden.

This chapter shows how to make something special of gates and doors, fences, walls and hedges, pathways, ponds and streams, planted containers, garden furnishings and outbuildings. It also reveals the most effective way to include features in the cottage garden. A little thought and a light hand will give you the most appropriate, subtle results for enhancing your cottage garden.

GATES & DOORS

ALTHOUGH COTTAGERS PROBABLY never gave them much thought, gates and doors are important features of cottage gardens. The gate allows an enticing glimpse of the garden, while the door makes a powerful focal point.

The Function of Gates

In the past, the gate kept farm animals out of the garden and today in the country it still serves this purpose. In addition, it has become a decorative feature in its own right, and, although people rarely pay much attention to gates, being more interested in what they see over or through them, the garden gate should be carefully planned to blend harmoniously with the fence, wall or hedge.

Most gates are found at the head of the main path that leads from the road to the front door, but there are usually some other gates, often tucked away or half hidden, that lead to the surrounding fields or to the farm. These gates are mostly of a rustic nature as they serve more a functional than decorative role.

In rural areas, where there is a good chance of obtaining farmyard manure, it is useful to incorporate a farm gate in the fence, hedge or wall, so that a

FRAMED DOORWAY Climbing ivy, Hedera colchica *'Dentata Variegata', frames the door of this garden shed.*

TRADITIONAL WICKET GATE Set in a Lonicera nitida *hedge, this is one of the most common of gates.*

trailer can back into the garden from the field. Throwing manure over a hedge or barrowing it through the front gate can be very tiring, not to say messy, and being able to tip it from the trailer directly into the garden saves a lot of energy and trouble.

Wooden & Metal Gates

The simplest type of gateway is a hole in the hedge filled with a white wooden gate. Its beauty lies in its simple and discreet nature – it draws little attention away from the garden beyond. Sadly, in cottage gardens you often see the gate in a dilapidated state, hanging from one hinge and usually lodged open. It is much more useful if both hinges on the gate are in working order and if the gate itself is well protected with a good coat of white paint.

In cottage gardens with brick or stone walls, metal gates are popular. Made by the local blacksmith or discarded from larger houses, they are usually simple in design and painted black or left to take on the natural brown patina of rust.

Embellishing Gates

Try building a rustic arch with poles and cover it with untidy scramblers such as roses to give the gate a cheery, informal air. Alternatively, let the hedge

GARDEN DOOR Not all doorways have to be ancient and decrepit to give atmosphere to a cottage, but it helps. Beside this doorway are the contrasting vivid yellow and bright blue of a laburnum and a ceanothus.

DOOR ORNAMENT Many cottagers hang horseshoes on or next to the door to bring good luck to the household. Hang them with the opening at the top so that the luck does not run out.

grow taller at the gateway and then bend it over to form a clipped archway to provide a simple but attractive gateway, which works particularly well when combined with topiary. Of course, you could incorporate a more formal archway constructed of stone, brick or wrought iron.

Cottage Doors

Standing in the road outside the classic cottage garden, you can see over the garden gate, down the path flanked with flower beds, to the front door of the cottage. The door is a simple affair, constructed of planks of wood in keeping with the style of the

cottage. The simplest doors are usually made of planks. Doors made of oak are often treated with linseed oil while other woods suit the cottage better when they have a coat of paint. Cottage doors I remember as a child always seemed to be peeling and of an indeterminate, subtle colour. It is only with the advent of modern paints that we have such a wide range of, often bright, colours to choose from. As the cottage door will be the obvious focal point at the end of the path, do not over-emphasize it by painting the door too bright a colour. Instead, give subtle emphasis around the door with plants.

Framing Doors

Roses around the front door epitomize the country-cottage style, and the view through a gate or a door wreathed in pink or yellow roses will send passers-by into raptures. Climbing roses can be grown against the wall around the door or, if you have one, over a porch for a more three-dimensional look. The variety of roses to choose from is enormous but as the odd branch always hangs loose, it is wise to choose one of the thornless varieties. A good choice is *Rosa* 'Zéphirine Drouhin', which is repeat-flowering, producing a fragrant display for most of the summer. Honeysuckle too can be used to great effect around the front door. In fact, virtually any climber or creeper – for example, clematis, wisteria or one of the vines – can look good.

Statuesque hollyhocks guarding the front door is another image conjured up when speaking of the cottage garden. Avoid the modern, dumpy cultivars and opt for the old-fashioned, tall varieties.

Another cottagey concept is to grow stonecrops or houseleeks on the front porch. The yellow *Sedum acre* gives a splendid display in the summer. Apply a slurry of cow manure to the tiles and insert a few pieces of stonecrop and houseleek, securing them with a little wire. They will soon form a dense mat and spread across the porch. As they do so, lichen will be attracted, adding extra colour and texture.

From Cottage to Garden

As the cottager steps outside the front door, he sees and smells the garden and stops to absorb it. Consequently, the favourite place for a bench has always been beside the front door. To enjoy fully such a position, plant your favourite fragrant plants near the doorway to greet you as you go in and out of the cottage and to savour when you sit outside.

FENCES, WALLS & HEDGES

BARRIERS SERVE THREE PURPOSES: they mark the cottage's boundary, defend it and provide privacy. In the country a stock-proof barrier is essential to prevent sheep and cattle from straying into the garden and the seclusion an enclosure provides turns your garden into a private haven.

The most suitable type of boundary for a cottage garden depends on the location of the cottage, and on the depth of your pocket. In areas where there are large quantities of stone available, walls are likely to be common. In the past, they were cheap. Nowadays, even if stone is readily available, it is expensive to have a stone wall built. Away from stone-producing areas, walls are not generally found around cottages as the cost of transporting stones has always been very high. In these areas you are more likely to find hedges or fences.

WILLOW WITHIES (below left) A simple, home-made fence constructed from willow withies makes a practical barrier for enclosing the vegetable plot.

ORNAMENTAL FENCE A traditional iron railing with its wonderful, rusty patina borders the front of the garden.

——— *Fences* ———

Palings are the traditional fence in most parts of England. Chestnut palings are best as they are stock-proof and help to keep out the wind and, once they have weathered, take on a country air. Nowadays palings have often been replaced with spikes supporting sheep or pig netting, or, if you are

unlucky, just strands of barbed wire. True, they keep the sheep out but they do not reduce wind speeds or improve the romantic appeal of your garden.

Too expensive to use for the whole garden perhaps, but a fence that looks very much at home along the front of the cottage is a white picket fence. Similarly, the hoop-topped metal fences that you can still see occasionally look very attractive. For the traditional look, plant along the fences so that flowers push through them.

Wattle panels traditionally were used on farms for folding sheep, but in recent years they have been found more in gardens. Unfortunately, the decline in their traditional use has led to a drop in production, resulting in a vast increase in price. Few people can afford to fence the whole of their garden in wattle nor would that be particularly desirable as it forms a rather solid barrier and has a relatively short lifespan. However, it is marvellous for creating screens where needed; for example, a couple of panels easily hide the dustbins or compost heap.

Walls

Lucky are those who have walls around their gardens. Traditionally they are found only in regions where stone is plentiful, although occasionally you will see a brick wall around a cottage. Much as I love brick walls, it is stone walls that make a cottage garden, particularly those in which it is possible to grow a wide range of colourful plants. Although walls are expensive, they last more than one lifetime. Always use local stone and avoid at all costs reconstituted stone, as it looks artificial and comes in the most awful colours. Sandstone makes a warm, mellow wall, while limestone is bleaker but nonetheless handsome particularly as a backdrop to flowering plants and colourful foliage.

AGED BRICK WALL (above right) This brick wall has acquired a colourful patina of lichen and mosses, which make a wonderful backdrop for other plants that grow on it, such as this fragrant climbing rose, Rosa sinica *'Anemone'.*

STONE WALL Ferns and other shade-loving plants have made this stone wall their home. Many wall plants will gently self-sow over the years. When planting a wall, take care not to damage it by gouging large holes.

Most cottage-garden walls are relatively low but occasionally they might soar to 15ft (4.5m) or so. Shorter walls are useful for supporting a selection of small plants, but taller walls, including those of the cottage itself, can be clothed in a wide range of creepers and climbers. Sunny walls are particularly useful for sheltering more tender plants such as fuchsias and for fruit such as cherry trees.

Hedges

Hedges are the commonest type of boundary. They are relatively cheap to create and, if maintained, form a good, stock-proof barrier. They not only keep animals out, but also protect the garden from wind. Hedges form one of the best defences against wind because they allow some wind to filter through, thus preventing the turbulence that occurs with solid walls. The final advantage of a hedge is that it forms a wonderful backdrop for the garden.

Naturally there are disadvantages to hedges, the largest being that they need maintaining. For, although they do not require cutting as frequently as their town relations, they still need to be trimmed once or twice a year, depending on how tidy-minded you are. Another disadvantage is that they are not instant; it takes some years after planting before a hedge reaches maturity. Unfortunately, there is no such thing as a hedge that grows quickly to the desired height and then slows down or even stops growing. A good compromise is to put up a sheep netting fence and grow a hedge beside it.

NATURAL GATEPOSTS (below right) Two outsized, topiaried gateposts guard the entrance to this garden. Cottagers have long been fond of topiary.

IN FULL GLORY This Pyracantha atalantioides *is in its full autumn glory, covered in brilliant red berries.*

Many of the oldest hedges are a mix of native shrubs and trees. The older the hedge, the more diverse the plants it includes. In mine are hawthorn, hazel, beech, privet, oak, bullace, holly, box, honeysuckle and many odds and ends, including blackberries and wild roses. Such a mixture forms an interesting tapestry but tidy it is not. Even when trimmed, the varying densities give it an untidy appearance, but it is a wonderful hedge for all that. It takes a long time for such a hedge to become established as the various plants take differing lengths of time to reach maturity.

In the past, most mixed hedges started as a single type and subsequently had others added by nature and man. A frequent addition to the hedgerow was a fruit- or nut-bearing tree. Damsons were very popular and are still seen in cottage hedges.

The traditional hedge in most parts of the country is hawthorn because it is fast-growing and stock-proof. It needs trimming twice a year, although one trim will do if you do not mind a shaggy look.

Many other shrubs, such as thuja, yew, privet, hornbeam and holly, may be used in a hedge but bear in mind their relation to the cottage garden.

PONDS, STREAMS & DITCHES

O THE COTTAGER, ponds, streams and ditches were utilitarian rather than decorative. However, whether utilitarian or not, water adds another dimension to the cottage garden. The restlessness of water with its constant movement, reflections and evocative sound adds a quality to the garden that few people fail to enjoy. That, together with the air of informality that waterside planting conveys and the wildlife water attracts, fits in perfectly with the cottage garden.

Ponds

A pond was necessary to the cottager for watering animals and, although one would have been most welcome if it fell naturally within the boundaries of the garden, cottagers were quite happy to use the communal pond on the village green. The small number of ponds that were dug by cottagers were for keeping a few ducks or geese or to provide a store of water for the garden.

One drawback of the well-constructed pond is that it does not leak. So 1ft (30cm) away from the pond the soil can be as dry as a bone and totally unsuitable for waterside plants. One way to overcome this problem is to incorporate overflows that allow water to spill over from time to time into specially constructed borders that are filled with a generous amount of humus. These borders retain the moisture that waterside plants need.

Streams

It must be wonderful to have a stream running through the garden, but few of us are lucky enough to have one. I would be reluctant to suggest that you try to construct one as an artificial watercourse is rather grand and when not in use it looks desolate. If you have a natural stream, either plant it with native plants (grown from seed collected from the country-side) or with cottagey waterside plants of which there are many to choose from.

There are problems associated with gardens that have streams, the most devastating of which is the havoc wrought during or after a storm when the stream is in full spate. The gardener must expect the water level to rise dramatically and the strong currents to wash away many of the plants from time to time. Fortunately, water plants are adapted to recolonize quickly after floods and they soon recover, providing they have not been completely swept away downstream. In some cases, you may be able to create a diversion around the garden that takes away excess water in times of flooding.

Ditches

Ditches have always been a common way of draining the land in the country and one is often found around the boundary of a cottage garden where it prevents water from draining off the surrounding fields and flowing under the cottage. My own cottage was very damp until I cleared out the perimeter ditch which had become overgrown over the years. Such a ditch does not usually carry water all year round except in very wet years, but it always retains some residual moisture, providing an ideal environment for water-loving plants.

Many gardens have a very damp area that never quite dries out. If it is to one side of the garden or in a corner then use it to advantage by planting it with marsh plants that enjoy such conditions.

Waterside Plantings

A vast range of plants is suitable for waterside planting in or around its margins, many of which are derived from native species. Water plants are likely to spread quite rapidly, forming a dense mat or a mass of stems which not only inhibits the free passage of water but catches flotsam and silt, further blocking the pond, stream or ditch. This means that every few years it may be necessary to clean out completely the whole stream, pond, or ditch and replant. This involves a lot of work so think carefully before you take it on, although if you can manage the main-tenance, you will be rewarded with a wonderful permanent feature for your garden.

COTTAGE STREAM *The sound of a stream and the lush growth on its banks complement the cottage garden.*

PATHWAYS

IN THE COTTAGE GARDEN, PATHWAYS are more than just surfaces to walk on. They give shape to the garden, leading you through it and separating it into different segments. Pathways also provide a wonderful setting for the many edging plants that tend to flop over it with all of the typical exuberance of the cottage garden.

Main & Secondary Paths

People have a natural tendency to take the shortest route to their destination, especially in wet weather, as anyone with an L-shaped path to the front door knows. Most cottagers made the path from the gate to the front door straight. They also usually made sure it was wide, say a generous 3ft (90cm) across. This is because, in the cottage garden, the edging plants tend to flop across the path, cutting into the walking space considerably. If you make the path wide enough to start with, you will not have to struggle up a path with wet plants catching at your ankles – a very quick way to get wet feet.

WEATHERED CONCRETE Given time, concrete paths can take on an air of respectability as dirt and dust softens the new appearance. Here a secondary path, edged with rugged local flints, winds amongst the flower beds.

Secondary paths are there to show you around the garden, so they wander here and there, curving around areas of interest. One of the greatest pleasures of gardening is to walk about the garden with a friend looking at and discussing the plants. This occupation is all the more enjoyable if the path is wide enough for you to walk side by side rather than talking to your friend over your shoulder. A comfortable width is about 4ft (1.2m), rather wide for a small cottage garden but a luxury you can afford in a larger

STEPPING STONES In the borders, slabs or pieces of stone make ideal stepping stones for the occasional incursion to weed or deadhead.

COBBLED PATHS Local stones make wonderful cobbled paths but, because of their uneven surfaces, they are best reserved for secondary paths.

one. Obviously, secondary paths can be narrower if necessary as long as there is enough room to walk along pushing a wheelbarrow.

Dirt & Gravel Paths

There is a natural tendency to use local materials for surfacing cottage-garden paths because they are readily available and usually relatively cheap.

The cheapest type of path has always been made of beaten earth. With time, these paths become rock hard as stones from the garden and cinders from the

fire are thrown on to it. Perfectly adequate in fine weather, such paths can become a morass in prolonged or excessive rain. They are most useful around the perimeter of the garden, where they keep back the weeds from the fields and enable you to cut the hedge easily.

Gravel is a relatively cheap and very effective surfacing material that has well stood the test of time, its soft, warm colour and delightful crunch underfoot making it popular. Such a path requires some form of low edging to prevent the gravel from spilling on to

the borders. Brick makes an attractive contrast, and wood or stone also work well. Make sure that you are generous with the quantity of gravel you use as gravel paths can quickly deteriorate into mud tracks if the covering is too sparse.

Brick, Stone Slabs & Concrete

Bricks make warm-coloured paths with an interesting texture and a wide variety of patterns. They look best and are strongest when they are set on edge. Make sure that you use only frost-proof bricks or the path

Edged Path (below left) This paved path is edged with an abundance of plants typical of the cottage garden.

Brick Path In autumn this brick path is lined with the seed capsules of honesty, the remaining flowers of a pelargonium and the curled-up flowers of a yellow eschscholzia.

will need replacing after a couple of winters, and avoid the regular modern pavers, which should be reserved for shopping precincts. Moss can be a potential problem with bricks, particularly in the shade. Use a proprietary moss-killer to keep the surface from becoming too slippery.

Stone slabs are now very expensive, even in areas where they were once relatively abundant. Of course, there is a large choice of artificial or reconstituted stone to choose from but most of them, particularly the tinted ones, belong more to a modern housing estate than to a cottage garden.

Concrete makes a sturdy, practical path for the vegetable garden. If you brush the surface while it is still damp you will uncover the aggragate, making it more slip-proof. Once it acquires a patina of use, the concrete can look quite presentable.

Old, weathered concrete slabs can look at home in the garden, especially if they have lichen on them, and smaller pieces of stone or even cobbles can make an attractive path. Remember, though, that these will create an uneven surface.

Steps

Steps are normally considered to belong to the grander garden rather than the humble cottage garden, but a cottage is just as likely to be built on a slope as any other building. Indeed, some of the most delightful gardens are constructed on an incline that is almost vertical, creating a garden that is a wonderful wall of colour. When building steps, keep the scale and style within the bounds of the cottage-garden image in which informality rules.

Material for steps should be strong, stable and, if possible, slip-proof. For stability, bed bricks on to a concrete foundation or problems are bound to occur within a short space of time. Large blocks of stone might be stable under their own weight but if in any doubt, bed them in concrete too. Worn stone looks better than new, but let safety be the ruling factor. If the steps are steep, add a handrail: although you may not need it, some of your visitors might.

Steps can be constructed easily from treated wood. Wooden steps are particularly suitable for a sloping path: lay logs across the slope and back-fill them with soil. You can make sturdier steps with railway sleepers, which are long-lasting as they are preserved in tar. Remember though that this makes them slippery in wet weather and unsuitable to sit on in very hot weather when the tar might begin to ooze.

PLANTED CONTAINERS

COTTAGERS HAVE ALWAYS GROWN plants in pots to brighten the interior and exterior of the cottage. They stood large terracotta pots by the doors and in corners of the yard, and placed smaller pots on the windowsills and window ledges. Often the pots filled the window completely with brightly coloured flowers extending the profusion of the garden right into the house.

Suitable Containers

Containers were not confined to pots. Anything that came to hand was used: old buckets, stone troughs, sinks, half barrels and even hollowed-out pieces of tree trunks. Long before it became fashionable in the 1920s to use troughs and sinks for alpine plants, cottagers were planting them up to add colour to their gardens. The hanging basket is a recent innovation but I am sure cottagers of old would have loved the informality they add to the cottage.

Terracotta pots suit the cottage-garden image perfectly but they do have one disadvantage. Because water evaporates quickly through the porous surface of the earthenware, the soil dries out quickly. To impede water loss, line the sides of the pot with polythene, or, when they are in flower, slip a variety of plants in plastic pots into the larger terracotta pot, for a continuous floral display.

Planting Up

There really is no limit to what you can grow in containers. Some of the most popular plants for containers are pelargoniums. Their bright cheerfulness is particularly effective on the windowsill or outside on the window ledge. Bedding plants are also often planted in containers, and many of the perennials grown in the flower borders can also be used to excellent effect. Chamomile (*Anthemis cupaniana*) for example, looks wonderful spilling out of a large pot.

Climbers, such as clematis or even roses, can be grown in containers next to a wall if there is no soil in which to plant them. Of course, large, thirsty plants like climbers need much more attention in a pot than they do in the open ground, particularly in hot weather when they need watering at least once a day.

Good drainage is the first requirement of potted plants: ensure that there are enough holes in the bottom of the container to allow excess water to run out, and that the compost contains adequate grit or sharp sand to prevent overwatering and stagnant conditions to occur. Because the plants are constantly watered, nutrients in the compost quickly leak out, so add liquid feed to the water once or twice a week in the growing season. Avoid soilless composts as they are difficult to wet if they dry out and the containers blow over easily because the compost is so light.

Make certain that the containers are secure, particularly those placed on windowsills. Even containers standing on the ground can topple over and cause substantial damage or injury.

INCIDENTAL DETAIL (right) Small, unplanned detail can add inexplicably to the atmosphere of a cottage garden. Here a houseleek spills over a pile of old terracotta pots, forgotten in a dusty corner.

RUSTIC CONTAINER An old half barrel is filled with an unlikely collection of plants.

GARDEN FURNISHINGS

ALTHOUGH NOT STRICTLY NECESSARY, furniture, such as benches, structures, such as pergolas, and incidentals, such as bird baths, can add the finishing touch to the cottage garden.

Garden Wells

Everybody associates wells with the cottage garden and it is true that most cottages originally had one. However, the wells of the advertising agencies are not the same as the practical working wells of the country. The latter, in reality, is a hole in the ground, surrounded by a wall, with a windlass if the well is deep. The thatched roofs and other bric-a-brac often seen on wells are superfluous. So if you do not have a

well already, steel yourself against creating a fake one as they never fit in naturally and if you do have one, keep it simple. Whatever you do, please do not have a garden gnome fishing in it!

Pergolas & Arches

A pergola may sound too formal for the cottage garden, but when smothered in climbing roses or honeysuckle, it fits the cottage-garden image perfectly. I remember a rustic pergola from my childhood, just outside the back door of my great aunt and uncle's cottage. It was covered in an old pink rose and underneath it was a bench on which we sat on summer evenings. My great aunt and uncle have long

ELEGANT PUMP (above) A well-maintained pump forms a striking feature in the garden.

FORGOTTEN WELL (left) No longer used, this simple well is now home to a shade-loving fern.

USEFUL FEATURE A wooden water butt is useful as well as decorative.

since gone and, alas, the cottage has since been gentrified. Needless to say, the pergola has not been allocated a place in the new scheme of things.

Pergolas and arches can be made from wood or metal. Metal pergolas and arches are more elegant than wooden ones, although it is best if the design is kept simple. Cover the structures with any climbing or rambling plant, but consider roses and honeysuckle first as these plants suit the cottage look best.

RUSTIC DIVIDER A rustic rose arch, made from poles, separates one part of the garden from another.

GARDEN BENCHES Simple benches such as this weathered, cut down, church pew make ideal seats for the garden.

Benches

One of the pleasures of having a garden is to be able to sit in it and enjoy its peace and beauty. In the past, there was usually a seat by the front door so that the cottager could sit and contemplate passers-by as well as survey the garden.

The traditional cottage-garden seat was made of two stout pieces of wood or logs dug into the ground with a plank placed across them. In areas where stone was plentiful, a simple bench was made from slabs of stone or slate. Although this kind of seat is easy to make and fits into the cottage garden admirably, it is not very comfortable. Hardwood benches are more comfortable and blend in well as they weather.

The range of garden seating available today is enormous. Wooden, metal and plastic benches are all abundant, although those made from wood are the most sympathetic to the cottage garden and those made from plastic the least.

Bird Baths, Trays & Sundials

Cottagers did not care for traditional garden ornaments, such as statues, large urns and fountains, but simpler ornaments, such as bird baths and bird tables, they did enjoy. Bird baths were made of stone or concrete, which can be aged by coating it with sour milk or a weak solution of manure and water. This attracts various lichen, which add colour and texture to the surface. Place both the bird bath and the table where you can see them from the cottage.

FORGOTTEN WATERING CAN Everyday objects, if chosen with care, can add to the cottage-garden atmosphere.

The more prosperous cottager might also have had a simple sundial. A sundial adds a touch of formality to the garden, which can look very attractive.

Uncontrived Ornamentation

A couple of terracotta rhubarb pots standing to one side of the door or an old watering can lying around will add imperceptively to the overall impression. These incidental ornaments are often the most effective in the cottage garden.

BUCKET OF FLOWERS Cottage-garden flowers in an old bucket make a spectacular display to greet the visitor.

FUEL FOR THE COUNTRY Birch logs and coal scuttles illustrate the cottager's reliance on fire for heating.

OUTBUILDINGS

OTTAGERS HAVE ALWAYS TENDED towards self-sufficiency, supplying their own vegetables, fruit and animal products, and only buying those items that they could not produce themselves. For these activities they needed various sorts of outbuilding around the garden.

The cottager needed sheds of all sizes to store animals, vegetables and fruit as well as all the paraphernalia that accrues around a cottage, including, as often as not, the tin bath. These sheds ranged from fairly solid affairs made of brick and mortar for keeping pigs to simple wooden constructions.

EXTRA STORAGE Cottage gardens need outbuildings to store tools and produce. Ideally, the sheds should be sympathetic to their surroundings. Here the cottager uses the outside as well as the inside for storage.

SHED INTERIOR The insides of old sheds can be fascinating places full of old tools and equipment as well as cobwebs and spiders. They have a distinctive smell, which is composed of a mixture of dust and stored vegetables.

Most cottagers also needed a fuel shed for their wood, coal or peat and this was usually placed close to the cottage for convenience. The most basic of shelters was a wooden roof supported by four poles, which was used for storing wood. This type of shed can look surprisingly attractive as the stacked wood underneath forms a wonderfully textured wall.

Very few cottages had inside toilets, instead they had the privy which was just a small shed at the back of the garden. Some have been converted, as mine was, into a proper flushing toilet. Authenticity can be

carried too far, however, and the privy is one tradition that need not be adhered to rigorously. I certainly have not reconverted mine.

A kennel was once a frequent sight outside the back door of the cottage. Usually it was a simple little wooden shed just big enough to allow the dog to lie down, but occasionally the builder seized the opportunity to be creative and added decorative details, sometimes as unusual and elaborate as Gothic spires. Sadly, kennels are less common now as more dogs sleep inside their owners' homes.

Greenhouses & Cold Frames

It may come as a surprise to learn that the greenhouse has been an outbuilding in the cottage garden for over a century. Despite its modern appearance, it has been used for growing tender crops and germinating seed for several generations. The only part that is relatively modern about the greenhouse is the aluminium framework.

A greenhouse does not fit naturally into the cottage garden because of its sharp lines and the bright reflections from the glass, compared to the heavily textured surfaces of walls, sheds and paths. To soften its appearance, use a wooden frame instead of a metal one and include wooden side panels so that the glass is not full-length. With modern preservation treatment, you can leave the wood its natural colour, although traditionally the cottager would have painted it, usually white or green. If you think that the greenhouse still stands out too much, try screening it with a trellis, which you can then cover with climbers such as honeysuckle and clematis.

There is no doubt that a greenhouse is a useful adjunct to the cottage garden. However, many of its functions can be carried out in the less obtrusive cold frame. A cold frame's only real disadvantage is that it is unpleasant to use in rainy weather: it protects the plants but not the gardener. It's advantages over the greenhouse are that it can be opened up completely in hot weather and can be insulated more easily in winter if necessary.

Beehives

Bees are an essential part of the countryside, pollinating plants as they collect honey, and quite a number of cottagers still like to keep them. Bees are often depicted in the traditional white-painted hive or even the old straw skeps. These skeps were very easy to make out of straw and split bramble. Of course,

straw is not waterproof, so the skep was usually covered with hessian or even an earthenware pot to keep out the rain. In fact, the skeps have not been used for many generations and even the white WBC hives are rarely used as they are somewhat impractical. They have been replaced by the "national", a much easier hive to handle, the honey frames being in a separate chamber from the queen bee.

The Pig Sty

Once one of the commonest of outbuildings but now almost extinct, is the pig sty. The family pig provided a whole range of meats and sausages and was cheap

Wood Shed A lean-to shed provides dry storage for the winter's supply of logs. No outbuilding, however humble, ever goes unused in the country.

Dog Kennel Working dogs are still rarely given the run of the home and are housed outside in all weathers in a kennel.

to keep as it lived on scraps and leftovers. Usually a substantial structure made from brick or stone, the most common type was a single-storey construction with ventilation slits and a door that gave out on to the surrounding exercise yard. A stone wall contained both pig sty and yard. Some pig stys were built to contain hens too. In these taller buildings, the hens were kept above the pig sty in the loft.

Chicken Houses

In the past, chickens were widely kept and, although numbers have certainly dwindled, many country people still keep a few. If it was impractical to let them roam free, the chickens were kept in a large run made of wire netting by day and shut in the wooden chicken house at night to protect them from foxes and the cold. Broody hens were kept in the chicken coop, a wooden box with a slatted front just large enough to hold a hen and a nest. You often see the chicken coop romantically portrayed with the hen's head poking out as she clucks anxiously at the newly hatched chicks scurrying about outside, tentatively exploring their new surroundings.

THREE

PLANNING THE COTTAGE GARDEN

The cottager did not consciously "design" his garden but was guided chiefly by common sense. He grew the vegetables in the best soil and in rows so that they were easy to pick, and the herbs near the kitchen door where they were handy for use in cooking. However, he gave some consideration to appearance, combining features and plants in a way that was pleasing to him.

This chapter contains six detailed, full-colour plans to show how to combine a range of features and plants to create attractive and useful gardens. Climbers and herbs, flowers for cutting, fruit, vegetables and livestock are all featured to highlight the versatility of the cottage garden.

These plans are offered as inspiration and can be adapted easily to suit the requirements of the cottage gardener. Although cottage gardens have a well-established, lived-in air, there is little that is fixed about them: the gardener can introduce new plants and features from year to year, so that his garden evolves gradually.

THE FLOWER GARDEN

THE QUINTESSENCE OF THE COTTAGE GARDEN is an abundance of colour and a jumble of scents. The cottage flower garden is crowded with flowering plants, jostling one on top of another.

There are practical reasons for such dense planting. Firstly, the leaves form a protective screen so that weeds have little chance of germinating and, if weeds do emerge, the dense canopy cuts out the light they need to survive. In other words, the plants act as a ground cover.

Secondly, the packed-in plants support each other, rather like drunks after a party. This reduces the amount of staking and tying that is necessary. In fact, in some cases you may want to let plants flop: for example, after cutting back a plant, you might want to allow the one behind it to flop into the space and fill the gap; alternatively, where the paths are wide enough, edging plants, such as pinks, always look pretty if allowed to sprawl out on to them.

The third advantage of dense planting is that it forms a microclimate (as in the steaming jungle). A layer of humid air stays around the stems, helping to prevent them from flagging on hot days.

Random Plantings

Cottage gardens are rarely filled with just one type of plant – they usually contain a wide mixture, begged or borrowed from other gardens or gardeners. A variety of plants helps to keep the beds free from diseases and pests as they have little chance of finding a sufficient number of hosts to become established.

By planting a wide range of flowers, you can extend the flowering season from winter right through to late autumn. In the first of the plans, *Focus on Flowers*, there are hellebores to lighten the winter days and Michaelmas daisies to brighten the shortening days of autumn.

Perhaps the most important aspect of this jumble of plants that we call a cottage flower garden is that it is incredibly attractive. In conventional flower borders, the plants are arranged in drifts for a calming effect. The opposite is true of the cottage flower garden. Random plantings occur because as a gap appears either the gardener fills it with a favourite plant or nature takes a hand and self-sows a plant. In either case, a cottage garden looks all the better for it. Mother Nature has an uncanny way of self-sowing two colours together that no gardener would attempt, which results in stunning combinations.

Variations on a Theme

Originally many herbs for medicinal, culinary or scented uses were included in the cottage flower garden. Gradually the herbal uses of many of the flowering plants were forgotten and they were grown simply because of the pleasure they gave. Who can imagine a cottage garden without climbers covering

GIFT OF SUMMER Early summer reveals a wonderful variation of colours and textures in the cottage garden.

BLAZING COLOUR Red-hot pokers, Kniphofia, *and the blue* Nepeta *'Six Hills Giant' dominate this cottage scene.*

walls, sheds, arbours, arches and even old trees in a wild, abandoned manner. You will find all these, and herbs, in the second plan, *Flowers & Climbers*. That said, the flower garden is an indulgence compared to the hard-working productive garden and many people cannot envisage a cottage garden that does not include some vegetables. Fruit trees are also a common feature in many cottage gardens, providing fruit to eat and shade under which to sit. In the third plan, *Flowers & Vegetables*, a few rows of vegetables and flowers for cutting have been introduced into a comparatively small flower garden.

Reflecting your Personality

A cottage flower garden is very personal and, although others will peer over the gate, it is essentially created by the gardener for his or her own pleasure. The best cottage gardens reflect their owners and this is why few, if any, continue after their creator's departure. It also makes it difficult to give more than generalized guidance on how to create a cottage garden. With these plans as inspiration, walk up and down the garden path, looking and thinking, and you will generate your own ideas.

One final point to remember when planning your perfect cottage flower garden is to avoid a rigid plan. When planting, pay attention to the colour, height and time of flowering of each plant but do not try to rule the garden with a rod of iron. It is much better to allow a degree of flexibility that permits the exuberance of such a garden to flow and allows Mother Nature to give a helping hand. Push plants in wherever there is a gap and if it looks right, do not worry too much about the "rules".

FOCUS ON FLOWERS

FEW SHRUBS WERE INCLUDED traditionally in the cottage garden and what there were usually bore fruit. However, several shrubs are well worth growing, particularly at the back of the border, where they help to form the structure of the garden. The subtle colour and perfume of shrub roses are well suited to the cottage garden, as are the much-loved fragrant lilacs (*Syringa vulgaris*) of spring, and buddleia (*Buddleia davidii*), similarly coloured but flowering in late summer.

Several herbaceous plants were widely used to give height to the border. No garden should be without the stately hollyhock, *Alcea rosea*, often planted next to the front door. Although perennial, it is best replaced every year and will provide more than enough seed, usually obliging by self-sowing. The foxglove, *Digitalis purpurea*, is another tall plant frequently seen in the cottage garden. For a natural look, allow foxgloves to self-sow throughout the garden and weed out unwanted seedlings.

Low-growing Plants

In this plan the front of the border edging the gravel path is devoted to low-growing plants. Allow some edging plants to flop out over the path for an attractive, informal look. In the spring, primroses, saxifrage and pansies brighten the paths, snowdrops provide a splash of colour under the apple tree and daffodils cheer up the cottage. Pinks have long been favourites in the cottage garden as they have an appealing fragrance as well as visual beauty. Unfortunately they often have a short flowering season, although some of the modern varieties flower all summer.

Other favourites include wallflowers (*Cheiranthus* 'Wenlock Beauty'), cranesbill (*Geranium sanguineum*) and bellflowers (*Campanula carpatica*). With a little thought, you can use edging plants to give a continuous season of flowering from early spring through to autumn.

Intermediate Planting

The plants placed between the low plants and the tall, background plants show how colours can be mixed and neighbouring plants selected in such a way that as one finishes flowering the next takes its place.

WALL FAVOURITES Aubrieta is a much-loved spring favourite and is shown off to perfection when planted along walls. Peering over the wall next to it is a bush of fragrant rosemary, Rosmarinus officinalis.

These medium-sized plants need not be limited to herbaceous perennials. Popular annuals to include are poppies (*Papaver atlanticum*), cornflowers (*Centaurea cyanus*) and snapdragons (*Antirrhinum majus*). Biennials such as sweet williams (*Dianthus barbatus*) are also suitable. Some must be propagated or bought each year, but others are self-sowing and sufficiently vigorous to grow alongside the herbaceous plants and take care of themselves.

Stone Walls

An old stone wall separates the garden from the road and a hawthorn hedge encloses the other two sides. Stone walls may be planted with a few drought-resistant plants, but, as such walls are often beautiful in their own right, this should not be overdone. Take care not to damage the wall by gouging out large holes for planting. Insert only slips of plants and keep them watered until they have taken, or better still, sow seed directly into the crevices by placing the seed on the palm of your hand and blowing it into the cracks with a drinking straw.

Plants that do well in this position include red valerian, *Centranthus ruber*, a typical cottage-garden plant (or possibly its white form), which is best grown from seed, and the Mexican daisy, *Erigeron karvinskianus*, which forms large, airy hummocks of small daisies that age from white to pink. I suspect that this daisy is of relatively recent origin but it looks the epitome of a cottage-garden plant. Once established it will gently self-sow. Among the most popular plants for stone walls are aubrietas, which come in a variety of mauves and purples, and, of course, wallflowers, *Cheiranthus cheiri*. If the wall does not get much sun, or is relatively damp then ferns can be used to great effect.

Hedges & Cottage Walls

The hedges here are of hawthorn, or quickthorn, as it is often known. This rapidly provides a thick, stock-proof fence that needs cutting once or twice a year, so it is one of the best for the country. Take care that tiny pieces covered with thorns are not left in the beds to impale your unwary fingers.

The walls of the cottage provide support and are a foil for climbing roses without which no cottage would be complete. There is a tremendous range of roses to choose from. If possible, select those with fragrance as well as good looks. There are many, including the thornless *Rosa multiflora*, which can be grown through an old apple tree, forming great domes of frothy flowers in early summer.

Overgrown Path By early summer in the cottage garden, the annual Limnanthes douglasii, *known as poached egg plant, spills over the garden path, while behind, white and pink dame's violet,* Hesperis matronalis, *sweetly perfumes the air.*

—PLANNING WITH—
Cottage Flowers

This cottage gardener has obviously indulged his love for flowers;
the whole cottage is immersed in their beauty and fragrance.

STORAGE SPACE *All gardens need a utility area of some sort, and the casual style of the cottage garden is better suited to it than most. But, if required, a trellis covered with climbing plants can be used to screen off garden tools and other equipment.*

TEMPTING SCENT *A scented lilac bush tempts the cottager to rest on the bench under the apple tree.*

WIDE WALKWAY *To enhance the natural look of the cottage garden, allow plants to flop over the edges of the path. Ensure that the path is wide enough to accommodate them and still leave enough room to walk.*

PROTECTIVE COVER *These hawthorn hedges provide a quick-growing barrier that protects the garden from wind and animals. Hawthorns are hardy, pollution-resistant plants that can be grown in any but the wettest of soils. They are particularly useful in coastal gardens where the soil can be extremely acidic and difficult to plant.*

SITTING ROOM *Simple wooden benches can be dotted around the garden. Here one is placed in the traditional position by the front porch. Another stands in the shade of an old apple tree.*

FRAMING THE WINDOWS *The dense planting continues even on to the cottage walls. Growing climbers, such as roses, clematis and honeysuckle, around the windows adds colour and fragrance to both inside and out- side the house.*

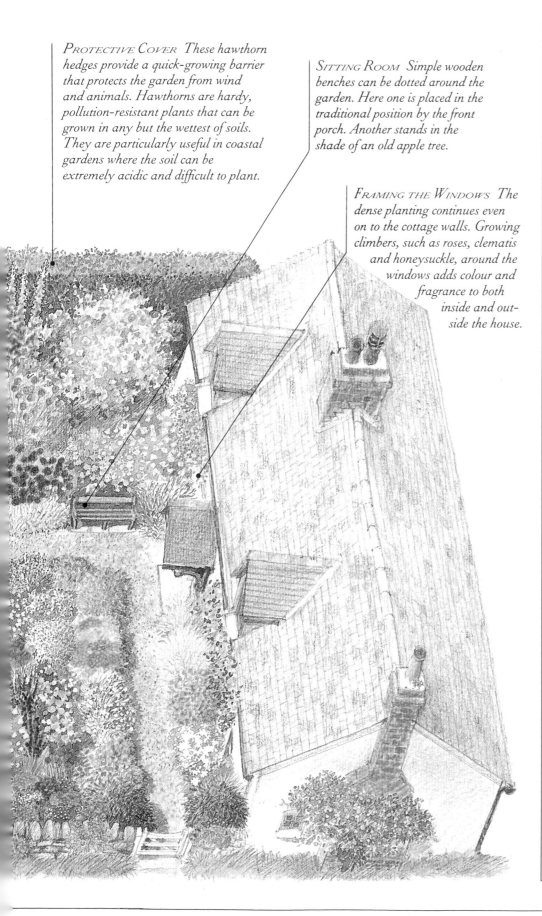

PLANT PLANNING

Structural Plants

Butterfly bush
(Buddleia davidii)
Foxglove
(Digitalis purpurea)
Hollyhock
(Alcea rosea)
Lilac
(Syringa vulgaris)
Mullein
(Verbascum bombyciferum)
Sunflower
(Helianthus annuus)

Intermediate Plants

Black-eyed Susan
(Rudbeckia fulgida)
Iris
(Iris unguicularis)
Lady's mantle
(Alchemilla mollis)
Lupin
(Lupinus *hybrids*)
Pot marigold
(Calendula officinalis)
Red-hot poker
(Kniphofia *hybrids*)
Solomon's seal
(Polygonatum *x* hybridum)

Border Plants

Chive
(Allium schoenoprasum)
Forget-me-not
(Myosotis sylvatica)
London pride
(Saxifraga *x* urbium)
Pansy
(Viola *x* wittrockiana)
Phlox
(Phlox douglasii)
Thrift
(Armeria maritima)

FLOWERS & CLIMBERS

ROSE ARCHES HAVE ALWAYS been popular with cottagers. Sometimes just a single arch over the gateway was featured, sometimes there was another at the head of the path in front of the door, and sometimes, as in this plan, there were several down the main path to the cottage. Occasionally, arches were extended a short way to form a pergola, perhaps with a seat underneath to provide a fragrant, sheltered retreat on hot, sunny days.

INTEGRATED PLANTING Variegated ivy clothes the wall all-year-round, tulips flower in the spring, and herbaceous perennials in the summer. Building up a garden in this fashion ensures interest throughout the year.

Choose the type of rose carefully to grow over the arches. While *Rosa* 'Albertine' is visually attractive and has a wonderful scent, it has vicious thorns that will rapidly reduce the postman to tatters. *Rosa* 'Zéphirine Drouhin', with thornless stems, is much better for this position and has the added advantage of blooming throughout the summer. For a more vigorous grower, choose one of the *Rosa multiflora* cultivars that are thornless but not repeat-flowering.

Rosa multiflora is an ideal plant to grow over the arbour in the corner of the garden. Although arbours are not authentic cottage-garden features (they were borrowed from some of the larger gardens), they fit into the style well and provide a cool, shady place to sit and perhaps eat a meal. Here the arbour is positioned to give a panoramic view of the garden.

The framework for the arbour looks best if kept simple, constructed of poles over which you can train climbers. In this plan the arbour is covered with vigorous-growing clematis, which provides a leafy cover in the summer and, as clematis blooms at different times, a succession of flowers. There is a wide range of climbers to choose from: some, such as the Virginia creeper (*Parthenocissus quinquefolia*), provide strong autumn colour, while honeysuckle and jasmine are almost as popular as roses for covering structures of all sorts.

Clothing the Cottage

The walls of the cottage in this plan are clothed with climbers. The lush *Wisteria sinensis* spreads attractively across the whole of the front of the cottage. No cottage would be complete without climbing roses, so on the more shady side *Rosa* 'New Dawn' has been planted. This is not an old variety, but it grows happily on a shady wall, producing pink, scented flowers over a long season.

Window boxes on the window ledges also decorate the front of the cottage. Here the brash, modern pelargoniums look splendid. Window boxes and hanging baskets are more frequently part of town gardens, but their exuberance is not at all out of place in a cottage setting.

Wells & Garden Sheds

In a true cottage garden, the well was a purely functional object for providing water for the household as well as for watering the garden, so if you wish to include one in your garden keep it as simple as possible if you want it to look authentic. The

SOFTENED DOORWAYS Doors often look stark, especially when the cottage is made of dark stone or brick. Climbers, such as wisteria and jasmine, can help to soften their strong lines.

RUSTIC ARCHES New arches can look a bit crude when first planted but they soften with age as the plants grow over them, hiding most of their frames.

gravel path surrounding the well is edged with low plants. Self-sowing plants, such as calendula, eschscholzia and poppies, are especially useful as they happily self-sow in gravel, which softens and helps the well blend with its surroundings. The first two are highly bred, but after self-sowing will soon revert to the natural form of the species. If you do not like their bright colours you can always remove them, although I think that the fresh, bright colours are charming and fit in well in the cottage garden. A more muted self-sower is love-in-a-mist, *Nigella damascena*, which will seed itself for years.

Cottagers of old would have had a range of outbuildings: a shed for storing wood or coal, a house for keeping pigs and chickens, not to mention the privy. The modern cottager also needs somewhere to keep tools and other equipment, so a shed can be found in the corner of this plan. It need not be obtrusive and, to soften its appearance, it can be covered with a climber or creeper, such as honeysuckle, clematis, climbing roses or the jasmine shown here, which will perfume the air strongly outside the kitchen door on warm summer evenings.

Planting Herbs

Herbs were generally mixed in with the other plants, but because of their culinary uses, the most common herbs were usually grown near the kitchen. So here the area between the garden shed and the cottage has been allocated to the growing of herbs.

In this plan, the bed is a small, handy cumulation of herbs for the gardener-cum-cook. As such it should be planted for convenience rather than visual attraction. A simple, informal layout is much more suited to the cottage garden than the more well-known, elaborate herb gardens found in larger gardens. None of the herbs are specified in the plan as the choice depends on the cook.

—PLANNING WITH—
Flowers & Climbers

This cottage gardener not only filled the beds with cottage flowers, but planted up a handy patch by the kitchen door with his favourite herbs and made beautiful use of climbers to drape everything in sight – arches, arbours and walls.

TOUCH OF ELEGANCE *Fragrant racemes of purple flowers give a touch of elegance to the front of the cottage. Choose* Wisteria sinensis *for the best fragrance and a good colour. This variety also starts to flower regularly from an early age, a trait not shared by other varieties.*

WELL PRESERVED *Traditionally, wells were a practical feature in cottage gardens, providing water for the household and the garden. Now they are retained, or built, for aesthetic reasons. They should be decorated with restraint, as they can easily be made to look too sentimentally pretty.*

FRAGRANT ARCH *Rose arches are a beautiful means of decorating a garden path, or of dividing different areas of the garden. For obvious reasons it is best to grow thornless roses over frequently used paths.*

SIMPLE WICKETS *Simplicity should be the keynote of a cottage-garden gate, such as this typical country wicket. The flower border provides all the fussiness that is needed to add interest.*

HANDY HERBS The most frequently used herbs should be grown together near the back door, within easy reach of the kitchen. Others can be scattered throughout the flower border and grown in the vegetable garden. Growing your own herbs makes it easy to experiment with some of the lesser known species.

LEAFY GLADE Although not a classic feature of the cottage garden, an arbour fits in well with modern ideas of garden design. A rustic, wooden arbour covered with climbers is preferable to the straight lines of a metal structure.

PLANT PLANNING

—— Structural Plants ——

Delphinium
(Delphinium *hybrids*)
Fuchsia
(Fuchsia magellanica)
Hollyhock
(Alcea rosea)
Hydrangea
(Hydrangea macrophylla)
Michaelmas daisy
(Aster novae-angliae)

—— Intermediate Plants ——

Cotton lavender
(Santolina chamaecyparissus)
Honesty
(Lunaria annua)
Lily
(Lilium *hybrids*)
Poppy
(Papaver orientale)
Red-hot poker
(Kniphofia *hybrids*)

—— Border Plants ——

Fleabane
(Erigeron 'Dimity')
Forget-me-not
(Myosotis sylvatica)
Geranium
(Geranium 'Ballerina')
Primrose
(Primula vulgaris)
Rock rose
(Helianthemum nummularium)

—— Climbing Plants ——

Climbing rose
(Rosa 'New Dawn')
Jasmine
(Jasminum officinale)
Wisteria
(Wisteria sinensis)

FLOWERS & VEGETABLES

THE PATH TO THE DOOR IN THIS PLAN is flanked by borders of lavender and at the gate by topiary. Pathways were occasionally lined with just one variety of plant rather than with the usual mixed profusion. In some cases it might have been a narrow ribbon of small double daisies, *Bellis perennis*, in white or pink, that linked and filled in between the other low plants at the front of the border. In others it would have been a more positive statement as here, where a low border has been created out of sweet-scented lavender. This draws the eye down the path to the door, at the same time restraining the riot of flowering plants beyond. This element of sobriety was not a common feature of the cottage garden but an imitation of a larger garden.

Topiary

Originally adopted from the "big house", topiary became a form of folk art in the hands of the cottager. At one time the shapes were sculpted out of fast-growing privet, but this is difficult to control and

SENTRIES Spheres of neatly clipped box stand guard at this cottage gateway, which is surrounded by the climbing Hydrangea petiolaris.

soon yew was preferred, as it requires cutting only once a year. In some cases the topiary was carved as part of the hedge, in others it was freestanding. The shapes themselves varied considerably: those less able cottagers kept to geometric shapes such as balls, others let fancy flow and created a wide variety of bird and animal forms – the peacock was one of the favourites. Recently I spotted a topiary teapot tucked away in a cottage garden, so obviously the tradition is still alive and flourishing.

Colour in Spring

Between the lavender and the herbaceous plants in this plan are daffodils. They create swathes of yellow in spring before the lavender extends to cover their dying leaves. Around the base of the yew topiary is a large planting of snowdrops that greets the visitors as they step through the gate in early spring. The common snowdrop, *Galanthus nivalis*, multiplies readily and large colonies soon develop, providing plenty to pick for indoors.

Cut Flowers

Flowers grown for cutting were often a feature of the cottage garden, both for use within the house and for decorating the church on Sundays. This tradition continues along with the custom of presenting bunches of cut flowers to visitors. The earliest flowers of the summer, and the most gratefully accepted, are sweet peas. These can be grown either in rows or through wigwams of peasticks.

Cut flowers are often grown in the vegetable garden but there is no reason why they should not be grown at the back of the flower borders, or, as in this plan, in an odd patch of land by the house. Here you can easily water them to ensure a constant supply of blooms and their delicious scent will waft through open windows or doors.

There are often such odd patches of land in gardens. If you are not careful they can become waste land and repositories for rubbish. All kinds of plant can be put in such places, including rhubarb or fruit bushes, saving space in the vegetable garden.

The Vegetable Garden

In this plan, the vegetables are planted in rows, in direct contrast to the rough and tumble of the flower beds. There is no dividing line between the vegetables and flowers: traditionally the cabbages and other brassicas merged with the flowering plants,

Protecting the Crop The cottager protects his cabbage crop, tucked away at the back of a bed of flowers, with netting. Unsightly though it is, netting is effective for keeping predators at bay and certainly is more acceptable visually than a string of milk-bottle tops.

continuing the decorative appearance of the bed. Even runner beans have a decorative and screening quality. No detailed list is indicated on the plan as vegetables not only vary from year to year but also change within the year as the crops are harvested. The greatest variations are determined, of course, by the taste of the gardener.

In British cottage gardens, vegetables are traditionally grown in rows rather than in the more decorative patterns found on the Continent. However, the latter has become more popular in recent years and such an approach can be incorporated into the cottage garden if you wish.

The compost heap is an important feature of any garden but particularly of the vegetable garden. Here I make no attempt to disguise it – it is part of the vegetable-garden landscape and, besides providing compost for the following year, it can be used to grow marrows or cucumbers, which flourish when planted on such a nutritious heap.

Flowers & Vegetables

*Many cottage gardeners feel that their garden is incomplete if
they do not grow a selection of vegetables as well as flowers.*

*UBIQUITOUS GARDEN SHED Every
gardener needs a shed to store his tools and
other odds and ends that the art of
gardening attracts. Climbers enhance a
shed's appearance.*

CLIMBING ROSES AND CLEMATIS

*FLOWERS FOR SHOW The sweet
peas seen here are grown for cutting
or showing. They should be
grown up wigwams of peasticks.*

*BENCH VIEW This bench by the
front door allows the sitter a view
of the whole garden and of the
road opposite while he enjoys the
fragrance of the scented plants
by his side.*

*DIRT TRACK The path around the
edge of this vegetable garden is
made of beaten earth mixed with
stones and hearth ashes. This is the
cheapest type of path to make, but
it is generally too muddy for
regular use.*

*SUCCESSIONAL SOWING
Planting short rows of
vegetables a few weeks apart
provides an extended season
of fresh produce.*

SCREENED COMPOST HEAP

TRADITIONAL IRON GATE

PRODUCTIVE SCREENING *Apple trees provide the cottage with some privacy as well as delicious fruit.*

BOLD STATEMENT *The path to the front door is planted with a hedge of lavender, creating a bold statement all year-round with its attractive silvery foliage and providing a seasonal splash of long-lasting, perfumed flowers in the summer.*

BRICKWORK *Brick paths are a fine feature in a cottage garden. The bricks can be laid in straight lines or in a variety of patterns. Be sure to use frost-proof bricks, and avoid modern pavers as they are too regular for the cottage garden.*

HEDGE TRIMMING *Cottage gardeners quickly learnt the art of topiary. The shapes created can be simple, as here, or they can be more complicated – perhaps in the form of birds, animals or even people.*

PLANT PLANNING

— Structural Plants —

Apple tree
(Malus pumila)
Butterfly bush
(Buddleia davidii)
Lavender
(Lavandula angustifolia)
Shrub rose
(Rosa rugosa *'Maiden's Blush'*)
Yew
(Taxus baccata)

— Intermediate Plants —

Bleeding heart
(Dicentra spectabilis)
Borage
(Borago officinalis)
Columbine
(Aquilegia vulgaris)
English iris
(Iris latifolia)
Sweet pea
(Lathyrus odoratus)

— Border Plants —

Daffodil
(Narcissus *hybrids*)
Marjoram
(Origanum laevigatum)
Pink
(Dianthus *'Pike's Pink'*)
Snowdrop
(Galanthus nivalis)

— Vegetables —

Beetroot
(Beta vulgaris)
Broccoli
(Brassica oleracea botrytis)
Cabbage
(Brassica oleracea capitata)
Onion
(Allium cepa)

THE VEGETABLE GARDEN

T O BEGIN WITH, THE COTTAGE GARDEN was essentially a productive unit, providing for most of the cottager's needs. In it he grew vegetables for sustenance, and herbs to flavour food and cure ailments, he kept animals to provide milk, eggs and meat and bees for their honey. The animals also supplied other useful by-products, such as feathers for the mattress and leather for shoes.

In the twentieth century the emphasis has changed, and the function of a cottage garden today is almost entirely decorative. Many cottagers still grow their own vegetables and keep a few chickens, but they are no longer self-sufficient.

It is often said these days that we do not have time to grow our own vegetables and keep livestock. For, although we work shorter hours than cottagers of old, we have many more activities further afield than the cottager, who was rooted to the spot. There is still a lot to be said for spending time growing one's own food and tending livestock. The freshness and variety of the produce as well as the sheer enjoyment of growing vegetables and fruit and caring for animals makes it well worth the effort.

Allowing Sufficient Time

The amount of space and time at your disposal determine the extent of what you can achieve in your garden. The space element is obvious but the time

HOME-MADE STRUCTURES Winter sunshine in the corner of a garden shines on a supporting screen made out of woven willow wands. Simple, home-made structures around the garden are very useful as long as they are strong enough to withstand rough weather.

factor can easily be underestimated. It is wise to start your vegetable garden in a small way and gradually increase the amount you grow until your available time is filled. Do not make the common mistake of starting new projects at the expense of those already underway. You will be happier doing a little well than a lot badly.

If you intend to keep livestock, do not overlook the fact that they need daily or twice-daily attention. You cannot disappear for a few days and let the animals fend for themselves. It is essential to plan from the beginning a back-up system of friends who will look after the animals when you want to get away.

If time and space allow, it is often easy to get carried away and produce far more vegetables than the family can ever eat. As with flowers, it is very

GARDEN PARAPHERNALIA Frost and sunshine encircle this collection of garden paraphernalia on a bright, cold day. Such piles of everyday objects fit in comfortably in a cottage garden and add to the informal atmosphere that is inherent to a cottage garden.

satisfying to have enough to give to friends and neighbours and, from their point of view, generally very welcome. If you have a constant surplus then you can sell it; fortunately, there is always a good market for fresh produce. Many country people sell eggs and other produce on a regular basis. If supply is irregular, it is surprising how much you can sell at your garden gate to passers-by.

—— *Creating your own Productive Garden* ——

The plans for productive gardens presented here show you three possible layouts for a vegetable garden and also show how to incorporate fruit and livestock. Use these plans to help you create your own productive garden, letting your particular circumstances and preferences dictate what you do. As with the cottage flower garden, there is no fixed garden layout to follow, indeed it is always changing if you implement crop rotation. The planting of fruit trees and bushes and the location of livestock form the framework of the productive garden and the vegetables create a moving pattern within it.

FOCUS ON VEGETABLES

THIS PLAN FOLLOWS THE CLASSIC productive cottage-garden design, with an ornamental flower garden around the path at the front of the cottage and a large vegetable garden at the back. Many of the older cottages were set higgledy-piggledy on the plots, but from Victorian times a standard pattern began to emerge that can still be seen in many council-house plots; that is, a small garden at the front of the cottage and a larger one at the back where there is plenty of room to grow vegetables and keep some livestock.

The Main Garden Features

The vegetable garden contains three elements: permanent perennial planting, variable planting and a utility area. The permanent planting includes fruit trees, bushes and rhubarb, which can be left undisturbed for years. They should be top-dressed annually with manure or compost, kept weed-free and, except for rhubarb, pruned; otherwise they require little attention.

In this plan, the fruit trees are positioned across the bottom of the garden, their branches spreading out over the hedge into the field beyond. The other fruit is placed together so that it can be enclosed in a cage or covered with a net when ripe to protect it from the birds. In the past, the cottager would have depended on a variety of birdscarers, such as scarecrows or the ubiquitous metal bottle tops rattling in the wind. Fruit cages may not be cottagey in appearance but they are functional and I am certain that cottagers would have used them in the past if cheap plastic netting had been available.

The variable, more mobile planting is composed of the vegetables, which change from one season to the next and from year to year. Although partly due to the changing demands of the kitchen and the gardener's quest for new varieties, this is mainly due to the practice of crop rotation. It is well known that crops do better if they are not grown in the same soil for two years running. This not only prevents the build-up of disease but allows the ground to be used to its optimum capacity. For example, parsnips dislike freshly manured ground, but they are more

than happy to be grown on soil that was manured the previous year for other crops, such as peas and lettuce, which thrive on it.

A utility area is essential for compost and manure heaps and possibly to burn the garden rubbish. You can move this area around the garden as you like but keep it tucked away from view.

The relative positions of the components of the vegetable garden are unimportant. With good use of space, while practising crop rotation and good husbandry, both vegetables and fruit will give satisfaction well beyond the kitchen.

Functional Paths

The basic framework of this plan is made by the straight paths that divide both the front and back gardens. Design manuals tell you to avoid straight paths, particularly if they divide the garden, but as purely functional features straight paths are appropriate in cottage gardens. The rectangular beds that they frame contain rows of equal length, which are most convenient to work in.

In this plan there are paths around most of the garden. This not only enables the gardener to reach both ends of the rows of vegetables without having to walk over and compact the beds, it also makes life a great deal easier when cutting the hedges. Another advantage is that it prevents weeds from the surrounding fields encroaching on the garden. Beds that go right up to the hedge often become infested by weeds before you realize it.

The paths of a vegetable garden receive a lot of wear, particularly when it is wet. Bricks are slippery under these circumstances and gravel sticks to the boots and gets carried away, quickly denuding the paths. Although it might seem sacrilege, concrete is the ideal material for this position. Brush it with a garden broom just before it sets to expose the aggregate. This gives the path a good, slip-proof texture. The surface soon becomes ingrained with soil and the harsh rawness of the new concrete disappears. The front path and possibly those around the sides of the cottage could be constructed with local material more in keeping with a cottage garden, such as brick or stone.

The Flower Garden

The flower garden at the front of the cottage is laid out in typical cottage-garden style, with many of the old favourites, including peonies, evening primroses

WALLED GARDEN In this walled cottage garden the vegetable garden and flower beds merge into one another. A row of overcrowded turnips vie with the neighbouring carrots for more space.

FORCING PLANTS FOR EARLY PICKING Large terracotta pots with lids were used to force plants, such as rhubarb, for early picking by hastening the growing process. Here one nestles among the frost-covered leaves of globe artichokes.

and sweet scabious. A new feature in this plan is the use of an old apple-tree stump as a support for a clematis. In the spring this otherwise uninteresting stump turns into a pillar of flowers.

────── *Vegetables & Flowers for Showing* ──────

Many cottage gardeners are keen to enter their vegetables in local produce shows. Most participate out of a sense of fun but some gardeners take the matter much more seriously and develop special beds for growing their prize specimens. They often place these beds near the cottage so that the vegetables and flowers can be observed and watered easily.

Although this plan is of two ordinary country vegetable gardens, they could easily be put forward for one of the categories in the village show: the best-kept cottage garden. In this plan neatness and maintenance are as important to the cottager as the quality of the produce grown in it.

Flowers are also entered at village shows. Some are just cut from the plants in the flower borders, others are grown especially for showing – usually in the vegetable plot. Rows of sweet peas, dahlias and chrysanthemums can often be seen adding colour to the greenery of the vegetables.

The challenge of growing better and different vegetables and flowers keeps the cottage garden alive and vital. The rows, although regimented, have great variation in structure, texture and colour, providing infinite variety and interest to gardeners. Why else would friends and neighbours wander down the garden path and spend hours discussing them?

—PLANNING WITH—
Vegetables

The dwellers of these two cottages have included flowers only in their small front gardens. The large expanse of garden behind the cottages is primarily for cultivating vegetables to sell at market.

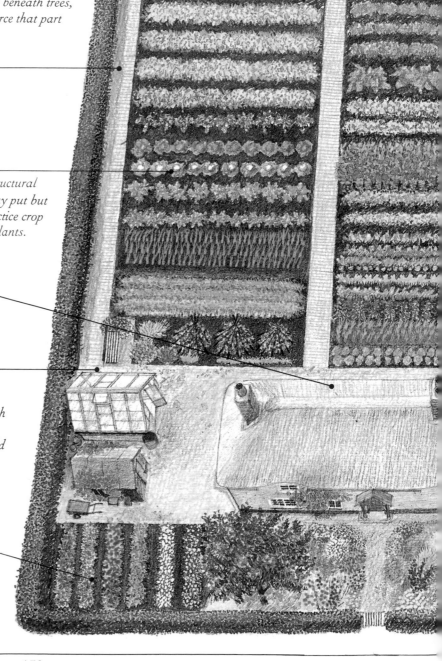

OVERHANGING TREES *These fruit trees are planted along the edge of the garden so that their canopy overhangs the surrounding field, allowing full-size trees to be grown without taking up too much space in the garden.*

FILLING IN THE GAPS *It is difficult to grow solid hedges beneath trees, so it is wise to reinforce that part with fencing or wire.*

PATHWAYS *All the paths in this garden are utilitarian, straight and solid. The main paths through the vegetable gardens are made of concrete, while those around the house are of more attractive materials.*

ROTATING CROPS *The structural plants obviously need to stay put but it is good husbandry to practice crop rotation with the variable plants.*

KEEN GARDENERS *Two neighbouring cottages follow the traditional pattern – a colourful front garden with a back garden full of vegetables.*

COLD FRAMES *One cottage has a greenhouse for germinating seed and growing plants, the other uses a cold frame. With the exception of a few tall plants, such as tomatoes, most vegetables can be grown in a cold frame, which is also easier and cheaper to keep keep warm in winter.*

PRIZE GARDENS *Many cottage gardeners love the challenge of the local show bench, growing vegetables and flowers especially for such events. In these competitions there is often a class for the best-kept garden; both of these gardens would be contenders for a prize.*

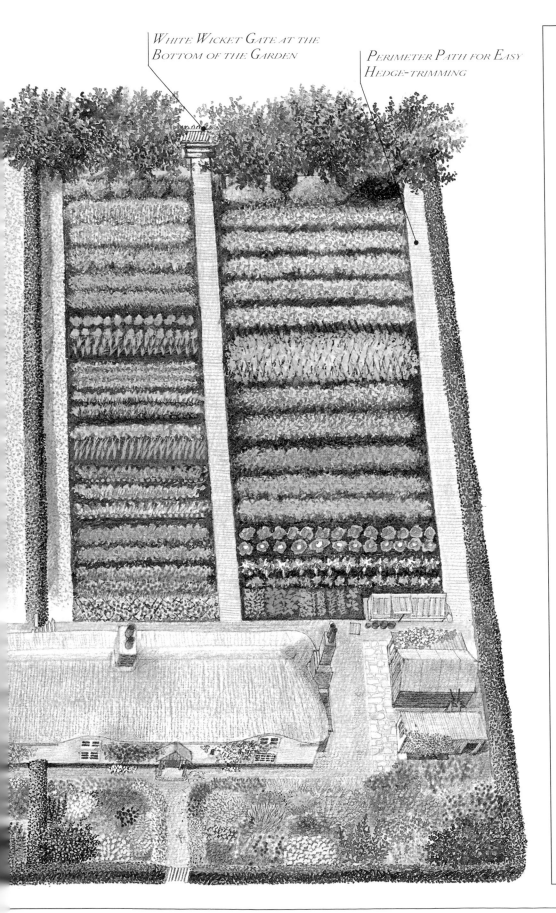

WHITE WICKET GATE AT THE
BOTTOM OF THE GARDEN

PERIMETER PATH FOR EASY
HEDGE-TRIMMING

PLANT PLANNING

Vegetables

Carrot
(Daucus carota)
Cauliflower
(Brassica oleracea botrytis)
Leek
(Allium porrum)
Lettuce
(Latuca sativa)
Pea
(Pisum sativum)
Potato
(Solanum tuberosum)
Spinach
(Spinacia oleracea)

Structural Plants

Apple tree for cooking apples
(Malus pumila)
Apple tree for dessert apples
(Malus pumila)
Gooseberry bush
(Ribes grossularia)
Raspberry cane
(Rubus idaeus)
Redcurrant bush
(Ribes sativum)

Intermediate Plants

Dame's violet
(Hesperis matronalis)
Peony
(Paeonia officinalis)
Sweet william
(Dianthus barbatus)

Border Plants

Candytuft
(Iberis sempervirens)
Snow-in-summer
(Cerastium tomentosum)
Wallflower
(Cheiranthus 'Wenlock Beauty')

VEGETABLES & FRUIT

THIS PLAN IS OF A LARGER GARDEN than the others featured in this chapter and is intensively cultivated to grow produce for market. It also includes a greenhouse. Cottage gardens have always had a number of outbuildings and there is no reason why a greenhouse should not be included if you wish.

The greenhouse is grouped with a shed and a cold frame at the back of the cottage, out of sight of the rest of the garden.

The Vegetables

In such a large garden there is plenty of space to indulge the vegetable gardener's insatiable desire for new varieties of vegetable in addition to all his old favourites. In smaller gardens this will be more difficult, although by practising successional planting and intercropping, you can grow a great deal of produce in a small space. With successional cropping, the ground is reused as soon as it becomes available; for example, when the early potatoes are lifted, the ground is planted with purple sprouting. With intercropping, the spaces between young crops are filled with quick-maturing catch crops. Radishes or lettuces are often sown between rows of young cabbage plants. They mature and are harvested before the cabbages require the space themselves.

The Fruit

Fruit trees are a must in the cottage garden. As well as providing fruit, they give structure to the garden and provide dappled shade. Think carefully before you plant trees because, once planted, they remain in position for many years. If possible, give them some shelter from cold winds and site them so that they do not overshadow the rest of the garden as both vegetables and soft fruit like plenty of sunshine.

COLD FRAMES Much cheaper than greenhouses, cold frames serve many of the same functions and are easier to keep warm in the winter. Use them for producing early crops or for germinating seed.

Some fruit trees that are not self-fertile need a pollinator: ask your nursery for advice. To save space, plant some of them in the hedge. This has always been a popular practice and you often see damsons and bullaces in old hedgerows.

The position of soft fruit in the garden is more flexible than that of the trees. However, it is a good idea to keep them all together so that you can tend them easily and cover them when necessary. Birds appreciate the fruit as much as people do, so if you want a decent crop, you may have to erect a temporary cage to cover all the fruit. Keep the plants covered only while they are in fruit. The rest of the year birds are a boon for controlling pests.

Bees & their Hives

Bees are a delight to have in the cottage garden. Old-fashioned hives (usually empty) are often included in "designer" cottage gardens to give them atmosphere, as if the plants did not have enough themselves. By all means include beehives in the garden, but include bees too: they provide honey and give pleasure as they buzz around the flowers. It is the bees that add to the atmosphere, not the beehives. The position of the hives is of little importance as long as there is sufficient room around them and the bees' flight path does not cross an area where you regularly sit or walk. You can place the hives so that the bees take off across a field or a little-used part of the garden, but do not place them in too exposed a position. In this plan they have been given a place beyond the fruit bushes, which they will help to pollinate, thus ensuring a good crop.

The Flowers

The flower area in this garden is more restricted than in the other plans but it still provides a colourful approach to the front door. More colour is provided by the rows of show or cutting flowers. Here cornflowers, sweet peas and dahlias are included.

One small feature of this plan is something that used to give me great delight as a child: a short rose pergola, made from rustic poles, with a seat beneath. Use a thornless rose or suffer the consequences.

BEEHIVES "National" hives are not as picturesque as the traditional white ones, but they are more practical.

COTTAGE JUMBLE In a cottage garden the vegetables and flowers are often jumbled together.

—PLANNING WITH—
Vegetables & Fruit

In this working garden, fruit is allocated a significant amount of land. The cottager grows fruit trees, currant bushes and rhubarb at the back of the vegetables and still has room for flowers for cutting.

GARDEN GATE *A field gate has been incorporated into the hedge to allow easy access for tractors bringing in loads of farmyard manure for the garden.*

BEEHIVES *Bees are as valuable for assisting in the fruit pollination process as they are for their delicious honey.*

FRUIT ORCHARDS *Most cottage gardens include fruit trees. Here there is a small orchard at the bottom of the garden. Those gardens with more space often have larger orchards in which chickens are allowed to run.*

VEGETABLE MARKET *An abundance of produce means that some must be sold, either at the gate or at the local market.*

WHITE PICKET FENCE

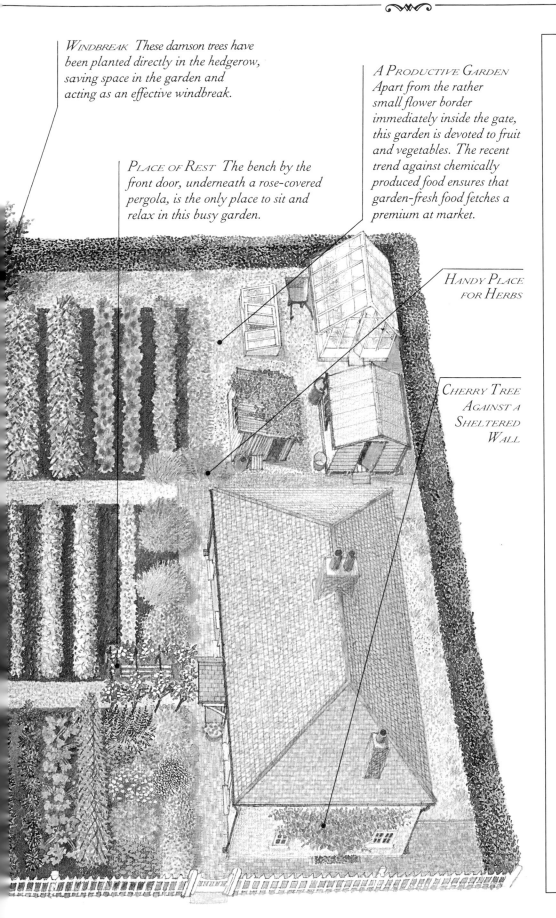

WINDBREAK These damson trees have been planted directly in the hedgerow, saving space in the garden and acting as an effective windbreak.

PLACE OF REST The bench by the front door, underneath a rose-covered pergola, is the only place to sit and relax in this busy garden.

A PRODUCTIVE GARDEN Apart from the rather small flower border immediately inside the gate, this garden is devoted to fruit and vegetables. The recent trend against chemically produced food ensures that garden-fresh food fetches a premium at market.

HANDY PLACE FOR HERBS

CHERRY TREE AGAINST A SHELTERED WALL

PLANT PLANNING

Vegetables

Broad bean
(Vicia faba)
Parsnip
(Pastinaca sativa)
Swede
(Brassica rutabaga)

Fruit

Damson tree
(Prunus domestica)
Gooseberry bush
(Ribes grossularia)
Rhubarb
(Rheum rhaponticum)

Flowers for Cutting

Chrysanthemum
(Chrysanthemum hybrids)
Cornflower
(Centaurea cyanus)
Dahlia
(Dahlia hybrids)

Structural Plants

Climbing rose
(Rosa 'Mme Isaac Pereire')
Lavender
(Lavandula spica)
Rosemary
(Rosmarinus officinalis)

Intermediate Plants

Bear's breeches
(Acanthus spinosus)
Yarrow
(Achillea filipendulina)

Border Plants

Ornamental sage
(Salvia farinacea 'Victoria')
Pink
(Dianthus 'Pike's Pink')

VEGETABLES & LIVESTOCK

THE COTTAGER DID NOT DEPEND on vegetables to keep him alive; he often kept livestock as well to supplement both his food and income. Nowadays it is no longer essential, but many people still keep livestock, either because they like to control all aspects of their food production or because they simply like keeping animals and enjoy the work they involve and the atmosphere they add.

Keeping Chickens

Chickens are still widely kept even though eggs are now cheap to buy. The quality of their eggs and meat surpasses any that you can purchase and are well worth the effort. Victorian paintings of cottage gardens often depict hens scratching for food by the front gate. This is now a little risky with the increased traffic on the roads. Moreover, it is difficult to prevent the chickens from eating plants in the vegetable and flower gardens, so it is best to banish this romantic image and confine the chickens to a chicken run. This should not be a poky enclosure – give the chickens plenty of room. If you have an orchard, incorporate it into the run.

Position the chicken run at the far end of the garden to avoid the occasional smell and the possible attraction to rats (they also enjoy farm-fresh eggs). Make sure that the chicken house is accessible so that the eggs can be collected easily. Be diligent in closing the chickens and ducks in their houses at dusk against poaching foxes and the cold.

Ditches, Streams, & Ponds

The most usual use for a stream or pond was to water the livestock and provide a home for ducks and geese. The sight of white ducks swimming or waddling about is very much a part of the cottage image.

Most cottages have a ditch running between the front hedge and the road, which is often dry in the summer. Use it as a decorative feature but do not allow it to overgrow or its efficiency might be impaired. Wild flowers such as marsh marigolds, red campion, ragged robin, fleabane, water mint, reeds and rushes all thrive beside or within ditches.

If the cottage is in a formal situation, such as on the edge of a village green, then the rough and tumble of wild flowers and water weeds might be frowned upon by your neighbours. More genteel in such a setting would be a planting of garden flowers such as mimulus, yellow and purple loosestrife and water irises (all "improved" wild flowers).

Waterside Planting

There are three types of plants that grow in and around the pond: floating plants for deep water, such as waterlilies; plants for shallow water that grow up through the water, such as reeds and many irises; and plants that like the moist ground at the sides of the pond, which include several irises as well as some of the Asiatic primulas.

SIMPLICITY REIGNS The simplest of bridges crosses this little stream, likely home to a few ducks.

KING OF THE CASTLE A cockerel surveys his domain from a vantage point that befits his status.

—PLANNING WITH—
Vegetables & Livestock

In this garden there is room for everything: an ample flower garden, a large vegetable plot, an orchard, bees, a chicken run and a pond for ducks.

BIRDS AND BEES Cottage-garden livestock is usually restricted to chickens, bees and possibly ducks, although some cottage gardeners keep goats. These animals create havoc in the garden if they are allowed to roam free, so separate pens are essential.

APPLE AND PLUM TREES

STRAIGHT AND NARROW There are two different types of path in this garden: the main ones are straight and above all practical, while the secondary paths meander through the flower garden.

THE DUCK POND It is not essential to have a pond in order to keep ducks, but they do enjoy one. Do not over-stock the pond or it will become fetid. Ideally a pond would have a natural flow of water through it.

WATER PLANTS Water adds sound and movement to a garden; it also allows for a completely different range of plants to be grown. In a cottage garden these must be carefully planned to keep them in line with the style of the rest of the garden.

ROOM FOR FLOWERS In a garden this size, there is plenty of room for a sizeable flower garden. Garden paths lead through it to the seductive lushness of the pond and to the hard-working productive garden behind the cottage.

CHICKEN COOP Position the chicken house against a fence, so that you can retrieve eggs from the nest boxes without entering the run.

KEEPING CHICKENS
Ensure that the run is large enough to prevent the chickens from turning it into a muddy swamp in winter, and that the wire is tall enough to keep the chickens in and the foxes out!

HAWTHORN HEDGE

PLANT PLANNING

Vegetables

Beetroot
(Beta vulgaris)
Cabbage
(Brassica oleracea capitata)
Potatoes
(Solanum tuberosum)
Spinach
(Spinacia oleracea)

Plants for the Waterside

Arum lily
(Zantedeschia aethiopica)
Hosta
(Hosta fortunei)
Japanese primrose
(Primula japonica)
Monkey flower
(Mimulus luteus)

Structural Plants

Foxglove
(Digitalis purpurea)
Hollyhock
(Alcea rosea)
Mallow
(Lavatera olbia)

Intermediate Plants

Cornflower
(Centaurea cyanus)
Japanese anemone
(Anemone x hybrida)
Yarrow
(Achillea filipendulina)

Border Plants

Lamb's ear
(Stachys byzantina)
Mossy saxifrage
(Saxifraga 'Peter Pan')
Poached-egg plant
(Limnanthes douglasii)

Do not use waterlilies that are too vigorous; only about a third of the pond surface should be covered. Other floating plants to consider are the water violet, *Hottonia palustris*, and the water soldiers, *Stratiotes aloides*, both of which grow in the wild.

Of the plants that grow up through the water, kingcups, *Caltha palustris*, are valued for their luminous yellow flowers in early spring. The yellow flag iris, *Iris pseudacorus*, looks good by a large pond. Forms of *Iris laevigata*, particularly the pale blue 'Variegata', are better by a small pond.

Among the many colourful marginal plants that contribute to the overall cottage effect are candelabra primulas, which flower in early summer, and the profuse mimuluses that add colour throughout the season. Most plants that grow around pool margins have an exuberance that is very much in keeping with cottage-garden flowers.

MAN'S BEST FRIEND Dogs are still very popular in the country both as pets and as working animals.

Domestic Animals

In the country, dogs were attached to a long wire that stretched from the kennel to the bottom of the garden, leaving them free to run up and down the garden path. Nowadays both the wire and the kennel are on the decline and dogs are allowed to run free in the garden and sleep indoors. Their increased freedom means that they can cause considerable damage, especially when young, but training and regular exercise will minimize this.

Cats are less problematic in the garden. Although they may use any newly tilled or soft earth as a litter tray, they need no special treatment or accommodation. They also serve a useful function by keeping both the rabbit and rodent populations down, which is especially useful when growing vegetables and keeping chickens.

EASY TO PLEASE Ducks do not need a great deal of water. Here a small flock is content with an old sink.

FOUR

The Working Cottage Garden

Looking after the garden all-year-round is essential to achieving healthy plants, fruit and vegetables. Arranged seasonally and using step-by-step illustrations, this chapter describes the techniques required to tend the cottage garden to achieve the best results.

Gardening techniques include organic methods of preparing the soil, sowing seed, lifting and dividing plants, staking and supporting them, combating pests and diseases, pruning shrubs, and making compost.

Country people have always been used to providing for their immediate needs and this chapter also provides mouth-watering recipes for drinks, such as cider, mead and wine, and a variety of jams and chutneys, all using produce that can be grown in the cottage garden. In addition, the authors suggest ways of using flowers and herbs to scent the house, such as pot pourri, pomanders and herb pillows.

TENDING THE GARDEN

IN REAL TERMS, GARDENING TECHNIQUES have changed little since the hey-day of the cottage garden. Some of the eccentricities and bad practices have gone only to be replaced by others, introduced particularly by those attempting instant gardening. We now have a barrage of chemicals at our disposal to get rid of weeds and pests, or to redress the balance of nutrients. Few of these are necessary if good husbandry is practised. The cottager's use of rotted garden and kitchen waste, in the form of compost, and farmyard manure if he could get it, helped to keep the soil in good heart. By not restricting himself to monoculture he reduced the chances of attack by disease or pests. Without the use of rich, nitrogenous fertilizers he did not produce the lush growth on plants, which is also prone to attack. The cottager made the most of what was already at his disposal: he worked with nature and not against it and this basic approach is still valid today.

Traditional Garden Tools

It is very difficult to find good tools these days. The shops are full of gardening gadgets designed to catch the consumer's eye but with little thought to their use. Unaltered for generations, the design of the basic tools is now deemed faulty. With the rise of plastics and ergonomic theory, we are now being told that we were using the wrong-shaped tools made of the wrong materials all along. So now our hands slip and slide on wet plastic, while edges dull with inferior metal. If you can, choose tools made from a good quality steel and with wooden handles (which can be reshaped to your own hands if necessary). Avoid like the plague tools made of aluminium: they are useless. If you have difficulty finding good new tools, look out for second-hand ones.

You will require a spade and fork for digging and lifting. You must also have a hoe. A Dutch hoe is used flat against the soil with a pushing motion, while a draw hoe has the blade more upright to the soil and is pulled towards yourself. A heavier, three-pronged hoe was always considered an important tool, but it is now more difficult to find. A rake is necessary for dealing with finer soil. Good trowels and hand forks are essential. A good pair of shears and secateurs along with a pruning saw should complete your armoury. Ancillary equipment that is useful includes a garden line, a sensible wheelbarrow (the traditional ones were made of wood, and these still look the best, although they can be extremely heavy) and a watering can.

Many of the large gardens had an extraordinary selection of tools, sometimes made to order by the local blacksmith. They often had specialized uses, such as weeding out daisies from the lawn, and were rarely needed by the cottager who could achieve anything he wanted with a small number of basic tools. In the early days of gardening this was more or less restricted to the ubiquitous heavy hoe, which would be used for all jobs from digging to weeding.

OVERFLOWING GARDEN SHED *This old garden shed is well-stocked with a range of traditional tools. Tools are very personal to the gardener and, once selected, they should last a lifetime if they are well made.*

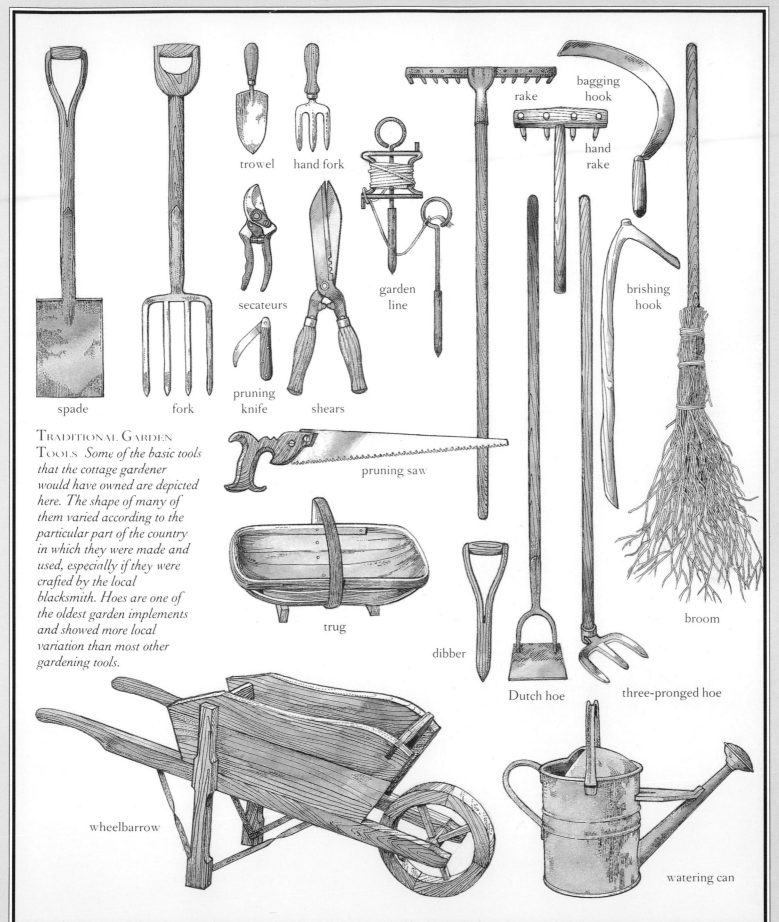

trowel

hand fork

rake

bagging hook

hand rake

secateurs

garden line

brishing hook

pruning knife

shears

spade

fork

TRADITIONAL GARDEN TOOLS *Some of the basic tools that the cottage gardener would have owned are depicted here. The shape of many of them varied according to the particular part of the country in which they were made and used, especially if they were crafted by the local blacksmith. Hoes are one of the oldest garden implements and showed more local variation than most other gardening tools.*

pruning saw

trug

dibber

Dutch hoe

three-pronged hoe

broom

wheelbarrow

watering can

Winter Tasks

WINTER IS GENERALLY A TIME of relaxation from gardening. Although there always seems so much to be done outside, the weather often confines activity to peering through the window in anticipation, and to reading information relevant to the garden.

Leafing through Catalogues

At this time of year one of the greatest of pleasures for most gardeners is poring over the seed and nursery catalogues that appear, and selecting the vegetables and flowers to be grown in the following season. Some gardeners grow the same varieties each year, often collecting their own seed from plants that have been left specially for that purpose, while others enjoy growing a few favourites along with some of the novelties offered by the seed merchants. Every year the different catalogues vie with each other in their presentation of new varieties, which they claim have a better flavour, shape or colour, last longer in the ground, or are more suitable to certain climatic or soil conditions. Most are highly illustrated with colour photographs, which not only whet the appetite and make one long for summer, but also, on a more practical level, give many ideas for plants that might be suitable for the type of garden you are trying to create. So, the hours spent looking at catalogues over the winter months not only give a great deal of enjoyment, but also lay the foundations of the appearance of your garden for the coming year.

Preparing the Soil

Many gardeners like to start their annual digging in the autumn, allowing the winter weather to break it down. Others leave it until winter or spring. With many gardens, if it is not done during the autumn there is no chance of carrying it out until the ground begins to dry out in the spring. Digging when the soil is wet and heavy does more harm than good. On light soils, and even on heavier ones when the weather has not been too wet, it is possible to get most of this done during the winter months.

If yours is a new or a neglected garden, it is important to remove all the perennial weeds. The easiest and most efficient method is to use a chemical herbicide. There are non-residual types available and, if used properly and the garden is subsequently maintained, they will not be needed again. If you are completely against using any chemicals, then there are two other possibilities. Firstly, cover the whole patch with a sheet of black polythene or several months and, secondly, thoroughly weed the ground as the digging progresses.

Methods of Digging

Once you have cleared the ground, digging can commence. Dig a trench and move the soil to the end of the plot. Incorporate organic fertilizer in the form of farmyard manure or rotted compost into the bottom of the trench. Then dig the second trench, turning the soil into the previous trench. Add organic fertilizer and repeat to the end of the plot.

Although not often practised nowadays, cottagers, when first digging a new plot, considered it a good thing to break up the sub-soil by double digging. Adding organic material to this layer helped to improve the soil to a greater depth, improved the drainage of the upper spit, and, during dry spells, helped with moisture retention. With this method the trench was kept wider than in ordinary digging. To do this yourself, break up the bottom of the trench with a fork and mix in extra manure or compost with it. Turn the next two spits on top of it, forming another wide trench. You can incorporate manure into the top layer as you dig. If your soil has a tendency to pan – that is, form a hard layer at a spade's depth – then it is sensible to double dig every few years to break it up. This is an old-fashioned technique, which has gone out of favour lately, more through laziness than good reason.

Winter is a time when you most notice whether the garden drains properly. If water collects in certain areas of your garden then it might be sensible to incorporate some form of drainage system; land drains are the most effective. These can run to a ditch on the edge of the garden or to a soakaway filled with rubble. If the water enters from land lying above the garden then dig a ditch along the boundary to alleviate the problem.

Different Types of Soil

Older cottage gardens often have a dark, friable (crumbly) soil, which has been worked for many generations and, apart from the addition of organic material and occasionally lime, needs little other attention. Lime is important as it helps to release certain compounds in the soil that the plants need; it redresses the balance if the soil is too acid; and it also helps to break down clay soils. Apply a light dressing of slaked or hydrated lime to the surface of the bed after digging and allow it to work its way down into the soil. Use sparingly on flower beds, particularly if you intend to grow lime-hating plants such as camellias, rhododendrons and azeleas.

The most difficult of soils to work are the clayey ones. These can be improved by adding humus, lime and either horticultural grit or a gritty ash. My parents' garden was pure yellow Wealden clay thirty years ago, but can now be worked with a fork in the depth of winter, simply because these materials were added over the years.

Sandy soil is quite easy to improve by the addition of organic material. While peat is useful it contains very few nutrients, and these are quickly leached out through the free-draining soil. Garden compost and farmyard manure are much better than peat as they feed the soil as well as bulking it out and making it more able to retain moisture.

Cutting Pea Sticks & Bean Poles

Traditionally peas were grown up twiggy sticks, often hazel boughs if available. These were also useful for supporting climbing flowers, such as sweet peas and some of the more floppy herbaceous plants. They were usually cut from the woods at the end of the winter, before they started into leaf. Similarly, bean poles, used to support runner beans, were cut at this time of year. Any straight pole would do, although hazel and sweet chestnut were the favourites. Modern equivalents are plastic or wire netting instead of the pea sticks and a wooden or metal framework with strings to replace the bean poles. However, twiggy sticks and bean poles still look the best in a cottage garden if you can get hold of them.

Add well-rotted farmyard manure or compost to the trench, spreading it evenly and forking it in.

Dig a second, similar trench alongside, transferring the soil into the first trench. Continue to the end of the plot. Fill the final one with the soil set aside from the initial trench.

DOUBLE DIGGING *This technique is an important part of preparing any bed. Dig a trench 2ft (60cm) wide and one spit deep, across the width of the plot. Put the earth aside.*

Break up the earth at the bottom of the trench by digging to the full depth of a fork, or spade. Avoid mixing the sub-soil with the top-soil.

SPRING TASKS

WITH SPRING, WHICH IN THE COUNTRY is heralded by a change in the weather rather than a date on the calendar, everything in the garden starts moving and there hardly seems time to keep up with the work. Many country people still get up with the light and spend an hour or more gardening before setting off for work. This is a wonderful time of day to be in the garden and early rising is a habit worth cultivating.

Finish any left-over digging from winter and break down the soil into a fine tilth using a hoe and a rake. Firm it down by gently shuffling over the surface so that the soil is not too loose.

Sowing Seed

One of the first tasks in the creative year is to sow the seed. You can either sow it directly into the prepared seed beds or into seed trays kept on a windowsill or in a greenhouse. You can sow the majority of vegetable seed directly into shallow drills, which are drawn out in straight lines across the vegetable patch with the corner of a hoe. Sow the seed thinly along the drill, rake back the fine soil across the drill and gently firm down. If the weather is dry make sure the drill is well watered. Do not forget to mark the ends of the rows. With some of the root crops, such as parsnips, which are going to be thinned out to, say, 9in (23cm) apart, you can sow the seed in stations, that is, three or four seeds sown every 9in (23cm), leaving the spaces between bare. When the seed germinates, leave the strongest seedling and remove the others. Country gardeners always like to make the most of space, so they often intersow a row of slow-germinating seed, such as parsnips, with faster growing radishes. This makes use of vacant space and the rows show up more quickly, making hoeing easier.

Some vegetables, like celery and tomatoes, and many of the flowering plants, you can sow in seed trays and germinate inside. Fill the trays with a sowing compost, sprinkle the seed thinly and evenly

SOWING SEED OUTSIDE
Most vegetables are sown directly into the soil. Using a line as a guide, draw out a shallow drill with a hoe.

Sow the seed thinly along the drill either by sprinkling it by hand or by gently tapping it directly from the packet.

Carefully draw the soil over the seed with a rake, covering it to the depth recommended on the packet. Mark the ends of the rows and label the seed clearly, adding the date.

Firm the soil down by gently tapping it with the back of a rake. In dry weather, water the row both before and after sowing and make sure the soil does not dry out.

over the surface and then cover with a thin layer of compost. Keep warm and moist. Once the seedlings have germinated, the plants can be hardened off by taking the trays outside for increasing lengths of time or by pricking out.

Pricking Out

Some seedlings are left in their seed trays and planted directly into the ground when they are large enough. This can lead to overcrowding and starvation. It is better practice to prick out the seedlings into trays or individual pots as soon as they are big enough to handle. The potting compost should contain humus: soil from the compost heap is suitable as long as it does not contain weed seed. Add some sharp sand or grit to help with the drainage. If you prick out the seedlings into trays, space them at distances from each other to allow them to develop freely.

Once you have pricked them out into the trays, water them and keep them in a shady place covered with a sheet of glass or in a frame. To avoid the necessity of pricking out, sow the seed thinly in trays, and pull out any excess plants, leaving the remainder to grow on in the trays.

Planting Out

You should not undertake to plant out seedlings on really hot days as they will have more trouble recovering. Space out vegetables at regular intervals in a straight line, using a garden line. Plant flowering plants singly or in groups to harmonize with the surrounding plants. Firmly plant all plants and then water them in. There was a tradition in some parts of the country of leaving certain plants, such as brassicas, out of the ground for some time before planting. This serves no purpose: replant them as soon as they are removed from the seed bed or tray.

Crop Rotation

For centuries it has been known that best use is made of the vegetable garden if the different types of crop grown in it are rotated. The garden is divided into three or four individual plots, depending on whether a three- or four-year cycle is followed. In one example, the first plot of a three-year cycle might contain peas, beans and salad crops, including onions. This would have farmyard manure dug into it. The second plot might include cabbages and other brassicas and would be limed and given a helping of bonemeal. The third plot might contain potatoes and

Sowing Seed in Pots
Some plants are raised from seed sown in pots or trays and then planted out. Fill the pot or tray with seed compost and gently tamp it to make an even and level surface.

Thinly sprinkle the seed on the surface. With fine seed it is often easier to mix it with sand for a more even spread.

Lightly scatter compost over the seed, covering it with a thin layer and then tamp it gently to level the surface and firm in the seed.

Water the newly planted compost lightly and do not forget to label the pot clearly with a wooden or plastic marker that you can write the plant's name on.

the various root crops that dislike freshly applied manure, and would be dug with bonemeal added a couple of weeks before planting. In the following year, the vegetables grown on plot three would move to plot one, which would be dug and have bonemeal applied. Plot one would move to plot two and so on. The following year they all would move on once more, and this pattern would continue as long as the garden were used. With a four-year rotation, the potatoes would be grown on a separate plot, often between the brassicas and the root crops.

PRICKING OUT SEEDLINGS
When the seedlings have two true leaves they should be pricked out into seed trays or individual pots. Fill a clean tray or pot with potting compost for them.

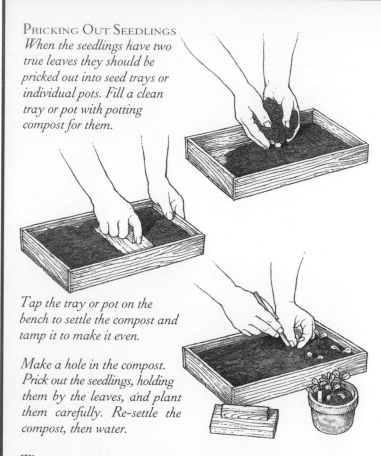

Tap the tray or pot on the bench to settle the compost and tamp it to make it even.

Make a hole in the compost. Prick out the seedlings, holding them by the leaves, and plant them carefully. Re-settle the compost, then water.

There would usually be an extra plot containing those plants that come up every year so are not moved, such as rhubarb and asparagus.

Care & Attention

Some of the more lazy country gardeners used to claim that weeds acted as a mulch and conserved moisture. Don't believe it! Regularly hoe or hand weed vegetable plots. It is a strange contradiction in cottage gardens that the flower beds give an air of informality and gay abandon, while the vegetable garden, into which it often merges, is strictly formal and regimented. Straight rows of upright plants with clean soil between them is the ultimate goal. I grow more shallots than I ever need just because I have loved since childhood to see them shooting up in their rows in the spring.

Flower beds can stay in place for many years but it is sensible to have a programme of renewal every few years in which certain areas are dug up, in rotation, and the plants split and replanted. Some plants, such as peonies and many of the tap-rooted plants, resent any disturbance and will either take a long time to recover or will die. These should be dug around carefully when the area is renewed.

If the borders are kept free of weeds and regularly treated in spring with a layer of well-rotted farmyard manure or compost, it is possible to keep them going for many years without a wholesale renewal, but many of the herbaceous plants will require digging out and dividing every few years, otherwise they will dwindle and eventually peter out.

The first reference to mulching dates back to 1657, so cottagers were well aware of its significance, although the modern concept of using peat, chipped bark or polythene was unknown to them. They would have used half-rotted straw or, more likely, a covering of well-rotted farmyard manure each spring. This not only fed the soil but helped to keep it moist. Watering the garden was hard work as the water had to be pumped or carried from a spring, stream or water butt, so watering plants would have been kept to a minimum usually.

Lifting & Dividing

Spring is one of the two times (autumn being the other) when it is right to divide and replant herbaceous plants. Although, in theory, once planted they can look after themselves, it is best to lift up

PLANTING OUT SEEDLINGS
Water the plants and then remove them from their tray or pots. Using a line guide and trowel, plant the seedlings in rows at the same depth as they were in the tray or pot.

Gently firm in the plants, adding a little soil if necessary. Level the soil and water them in. Plants for borders should be grouped in clumps rather than planted in straight lines.

most every three or four years and divide them. Some plants readily fall apart or can be easily separated by hand; others need a bit more force, which you could apply by prising the plant apart with two forks used back to back. Discard the woody central portions of the old plant and replant only the younger growth around the edge.

Taking Cuttings

Spring onwards is also the time for taking cuttings. You can take basal shoots of herbaceous plants, such as chrysanthemums or delphiniums, from the parent plant and pot them into a mixture of sand and peat, first removing any basal leaves. Water and keep in a close atmosphere in a polythene bag or propagating frame until roots form and growth of the shoot recommences. Pot up rooted cuttings into individual pots and wait until they are established and hardened off before planting out. You can also take cuttings from other shoots of both herbaceous and woody material and treat them in the same way. It is preferable to choose stems for cuttings that have no flower buds.

In many cottage gardens, propagation of such plants as pinks was achieved simply by taking off part of the plant and pushing it into a moistish soil out of the direct sun, where either it rooted or it didn't. Hardwood cuttings are done in this way even today. Take shoots of roses, gooseberries, currants and so on in the late autumn, place in a sandy soil in the shade and leave until they root and are ready to be transplanted.

Using Cold Frames

Cold frames and cloches have been used for centuries to produce early crops of vegetables and to shelter seed trays and potted-up seedlings. The cold frame consists of four wooden sides and a removable lid constructed from sheets of glass. It can be placed on cultivated land, and early crops of carrots and lettuce, for example, can be sown in the winter and harvested much earlier than those sown in the open ground. If the frames are put on top of manure heaps, covered with a layer of soil and sown, they will produce even earlier crops as the decaying manure produces quite a large amount of heat.

You can also use cold frames as protection for trays of germinating seed. They not only help by keeping the air warmer but also keep off excessive rain. Prick out the resulting seedlings into trays or pots and leave in the frame to gather strength. When

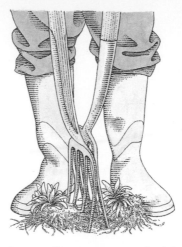

DIVIDING PLANTS *Most herbaceous plants need to be divided every few years. Water the plants thoroughly several hours before digging up. Some plants can easily be separated into pieces by hand, but others need to be prised apart using the backs of two forks. Discard the centre portion of the plant as this is often weak, old and woody. Replant the healthy, younger growth immediately and water in well.*

the seedlings are nearly high enough for planting out you can "harden them off" by gradually opening the light (glass lid) a little longer each day until they are open to the elements all the time. They are then strong enough for planting out.

Frames can also be used for such crops as cucumbers and melons, when extra warmth or humidity is required.

Cloches are sheets of glass clipped together or clear polythene placed over a framework. You can use these as small cold frames to produce early crops, such as beans or peas, or to ripen strawberries.

Staking & Supporting

Not all plants are able to support themselves. In the cottage garden the planting is often so close that they support each other. However there are some, especially climbers such as sweet peas, that need additional support. The traditional country way is to use pea sticks – boughs cut from hazel and other coppiced shrubs and trees. These are pushed firmly into the ground so that the plants climb up through them. In a windy area it might be necessary to support the sticks with string, or even wire, attached to posts at each end and in the middle.

Some of the weaker-stemmed herbaceous plants may also need staking, particularly in wet weather. It can be a lot of trouble, and the easy way is either to let the plants flop or to throw them out. If you are determined to keep them, in the spring push the pea sticks into the ground around the plant. Bend the tops inwards and interweave or tie, to form a strong framework through which the emerging plant will soon grow. With this homemade framework, the plant is supported against wind and rain while at the same time masking its support.

SUMMER TASKS

SOME TIME SHOULD BE FOUND in the summer to relax and enjoy the fruits of one's labour, perhaps on the bench by the door or under a shady apple tree. But there is still plenty of work to be done in the garden. Maintenance is particularly important because, if it is neglected, the garden will soon become overgrown and unmanageable.

Combating Pests & Diseases

Once the weather starts to get warmer, so pests and diseases become more of a nuisance. A lot of problems start when a gardener restricts himself to a monoculture, that is, he grows only roses or lilies. Then pests and diseases related to that genus move in and have a field day on the abundant host. In a cottage garden the diversity of plants tends to prevent this. One of the reasons that the cottage-garden plants that have come down to us have done so is because they are relatively tough, hardy and disease-free. The cottage gardener did not have time for weaker plants prone to pests and disease.

The worst pests that are likely to be around are aphids and slugs. Aphids (greenfly and blackfly) can be despatched by the time-honoured country method of squashing between finger and thumb or by spraying with soapy water. Although long established, the latter method does not seem to kill them but the jet of water knocks them from the plant. If the outbreak is getting too much, then resort to a chemical spray. Slugs and snails can also be controlled mechanically by squashing underfoot. A good time to trap them is at night. Many can be captured with the help of a torch, and then killed by dropping them into a jar containing water and a little washing-up liquid. They can also be found during the day hiding under bits of tile or bark. A vigorous campaign over a week or so should reduce the numbers to manageable proportions. Slug bait is the modern aid but, if you do use it, do so according to the manufacturer's instructions. Rabbits were another of the destructive pests that a cottager had to face and they still present a problem. Trapping and snaring was his answer but nowadays it is perhaps more humane to surround the garden with netting, sunk into the ground, to deter them.

Good robust plants plus good hygiene will go a long way to prevent pests and diseases. Clear up all rubbish, which will harbour them, and keep the garden weed-free, particularly of those that act as hosts to disease, such as groundsel.

Making Compost

Any green material, such as weeds and kitchen vegetable waste, should be composted. The traditional method of producing compost was simply to throw it all in a heap and leave it for a year. Occasionally a layer of farmyard manure might be added to speed up the process, but on the whole the cottage gardener of yesteryear was not in such a hurry as his modern counterpart. After the compost had been stacked for a year he might restack it so that the outside materials went to the middle of the heap, and then grow marrows on it for the second year, finally digging it into the ground during the next winter's digging.

TRIMMING METHODS
Traditionally hedges were trimmed once or twice a year, with a bagging hook, but shears or a mechanical clipper may be used.

Grass was also cut using a bagging hook or scythe. The trimmings were cleared away with a wooden rake or stick.

This method still works with great success if you are in no hurry and have space for two stacks. If it is more urgently required, you can stack the materials neatly with alternate layers of compost and farmyard manure, water and then cover with polythene to prevent moisture from entering and heat from escaping the heap.

Cutting Hedges

Country hedges are not cut as frequently as those in towns, usually only once or, at the most, twice a year. Field hedges are generally left till winter but cottage gardens need a semblance of tidiness and are often cut during the summer. It is also a good thing to clear out the bottom of the hedgerows before the herbage gets too rampant. By then most of the spring hedgerow flowers, such as primroses, are over and will have seeded themselves.

Weeding

Weeding should be a continuous process. You should hoe vegetables regularly but the flower borders should be handweeded. This may seem a chore but if done regularly, so that it is not necessary to have a panicky blitzkrieg, it can be a very relaxing occupation, particularly on a sunny day. Working closely amongst the flowering plants brings you a deeper knowledge and appreciation of your garden. If perennial, invasive weeds enter the borders, scrap either part or the whole of the bed and start again. It is a hopeless task trying to deal with this kind of weed with plants in *situ*, particularly if the invasion is extensive. Try not to use chemical herbicides.

Brick paths, especially those in damp shade, can get very slippery with moss. It may be necessary for safety's sake to use chemicals to clear this away.

Watering

There are quite a number of old country maxims about watering, such as, once you start watering you have to carry on doing so. Most of these I am sure were promulgated as an excuse for laziness. If the rain does not provide sufficient moisture then you must. Traditionally this would have been applied by a watering can filled from a ditch, pump or water butt. Water butts are still useful things to have around, and down-pipes from the roofs of the house, shed or greenhouse can be used to feed them. It is not only a convenient and quick way to fill a can, but the water is usually soft and of the same temperature as

the surroundings. However, it is very easy to skimp on the amount of water given by using a watering can and the only really efficient way of administering water artificially is by using a sprinkler attached by hosepipe to a mains water tap. Always make certain that the ground is thoroughly soaked before turning the water off or moving to the next patch.

Drying Herbs

Herbs were traditionally used for culinary and other purposes throughout the year. So that there was a supply during the winter months, many of them were dried. You should pick them in the early summer while they are still at their best, before the flowers have formed. Pick young shoots early on a dry day and hang them in paper or muslin bags in a warm, airy place to dry. When they are thoroughly dry, strip off the leaves and keep them in airtight storage jars, which are preferably lightproof as well.

HARVESTING HERBS
Pick healthy, unblemished herbs in the morning, taking care not to bruise them. Strip off the lower leaves.

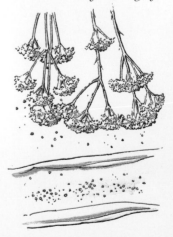

Tie the stems in loose bunches with string and then hang them, stems uppermost, in a warm, dry and dark place. They will need good ventilation to dry thoroughly.

Herbs harvested for their seeds, such as fennel and dill, should be dried in a similar way. Place a tray or sheet of paper underneath the herbs to catch the falling seeds.

AUTUMN TASKS

AUTUMN BRINGS THE YEAR round full circle. The produce from the seed sown at the beginning of the year is now harvested and the lush vegetation dies down to await the next year. It is also time to think of the year ahead by planting bulbs, trees and shrubs.

Harvesting Vegetables

Vegetables are harvested from the summer onwards. During the summer you usually pick them for immediate use. There is nothing like really fresh vegetables and you can pick them just before you need them. In former times there was no adequate way of storing the earlier vegetables. Peas and beans could be dried or salted to provide for the winter but the main vegetables for that time of year were the root crops. To ensure that there was not a glut of vegetables at any one time, successional sowing was practised, that is, short rows were sown at regular intervals of, say, two weeks. The resulting vegetables were then spread over quite a long period. Nowadays the easiest storage method is the deep freeze. You can freeze a glut of peas, beans, or most other vegetables for winter use. This makes best use of any excess and gives a greater variety of vegetables during the winter. However, all-year-round supply does rather dull the full appreciation of fresh vegetables that are only available in their season. If peas are only eaten when peas are ripening then they are all the more enjoyed and the same is true for other vegetables.

Lifting Roots & Picking Fruit

Root crops on the other hand have a much longer season. Turnips, carrots, beetroot and potatoes are available from the summer onwards and they are joined in the autumn by swedes, parsnips, salsify and several others. In drier areas these can be left in the ground until they are required. In wet and cold areas it may be necessary for you to lift and store them in boxes of dry sand kept in a frost-free shed or cellar. You should lift potatoes after the first frost and leave them to dry off for several hours before storing them in hessian or paper sacks (never polythene ones, which will cause them to rot). You can also keep them in boxes. Store them in darkness otherwise they will turn green and be inedible.

Brassicas should be left in the ground and picked as required. There is often a difference in the time at which they mature, allowing an extended season. Brussel sprouts, for example, can produce from late autumn until almost the spring.

In the cottage garden there always seems to be too much soft fruit to eat as it ripens, however much one feasts oneself on raspberries, strawberries and currants. There are several ways of using this glut. The traditional ways were to make jams, preserves or wines, or to bottle them. Jams and wines are still a popular method of utilizing fruit but bottling has dropped out of favour as it is much easier simply to put the fruit into the freezer.

Of the tree fruits, plums and cherries were treated as soft fruit and bottled or turned into jams and preserves. The hard fruits, such as pears and apples, were, and still can be, stored in boxes or racks in frost-free conditions. Periodically check and remove any defective or rotting fruit. Some varieties store better than others.

Collecting Seed

Most cottagers could afford to spend little on their gardens and the cheapest way of acquiring seed was to collect it. With beans and peas this was easy enough as they simply had to leave a few pods to develop fully and then dry off. Once the pod was sear (or dry) they would collect the seed and keep it in a dry, frost-free place. With other vegetables it meant leaving a few plants until the following season when they would throw up flowering stems and subsequently set seed, which was collected as soon as it was ripe. Potatoes caused no problems as a few of the smaller tubers stored over winter could be planted in the ground to provide the new crop.

These methods of collecting seed can still be done today; indeed many cottagers and other gardeners still do it (but do be sure not to store seed in polythene bags). One complication has entered the arena, however: with the complicated modern hybridization programmes, the plants raised from own-collected seed from some of the modern varieties may not be of the same quality as those that bore the seeds. This is particularly true of F1 hybrids, which will never come true from garden-gathered seed – the original cross has to be made again.

The same is true of flower seed. Many of the cottage-garden plants will self-sow, removing any necessity for collecting seed except possibly to give away or to exchange with friends. However, seed of some of the annuals can be collected and sown each year, particularly those of a tender nature. You should do the same with modern hybrids.

Preferably, seed should be collected on a dry day when it is ripe. Ripeness can usually be judged by the colour of the seed capsule and the readiness of the seed to leave its container. Some flowering plants have explosive mechanisms that fling the seed far and wide. Visit these plants regularly and capture the seed just before its violent departure. A muslin bag tied over the seed pods will capture it if you are unable to make regular visits. Once inside, clean the seed by removing any bits of dust or debris that you collected with it, allow it to dry thoroughly in an open paper bag and finally store it in a paper envelope or bag. You should not use polythene bags unless the seed is completely dry, otherwise it will rot. Store the seed in a cool, dry, frost-free place, preferably out of the light. When storing, always label the seed. All brassica seed, for example, tends to look the same and, if it is not carefully labelled, different varieties can soon become confused.

Planting

Towards the end of autumn, thoughts inevitably turn towards planting new trees and shrubs in the garden. These can be planted at any time between late autumn and the end of winter except when the weather is excessively cold or dry. The ground can be prepared during the autumn so that it is all ready when the plants arrive later on.

Dig a hole wider than the spread of the roots. Loosen the bottom and fork in some well-rotted manure. You can also add some bonemeal. Place the plant in the hole so that the soil level comes up to the same place on the stem as it did before it was dug up or taken from its pot. Spread out the roots over the base of the hole. Place good friable soil, with added compost if possible, over the roots. Firm down and

Place the tree or shrub in the centre of the hole and spread out the roots. It should be at the same level in the soil as it was when in the container or nursery bed. Check this by lying a stick across the hole.

PLANTING A TREE OR SHRUB
Dig a hole that is wider and deeper than the root ball of the tree or shrub you are planting. Work well-rotted manure or compost into the bottom of the hole. Add bonemeal to the loosened soil.

Refill the hole, with good friable soil with added compost if possible, making sure that the tree or shrub is upright. Firm the soil around the stem by carefully heeling it in with your boot. Water the tree or shrub generously and keep it well watered until it is well established.

Trees should be supported with a stout stake. Drive this into the ground before planting the tree, to avoid damaging the roots. Use a rubber tie to secure the tree.

water well. You should support trees with one or two stakes in a windy area, and also stake shrubs if you think that they need it. To avoid cutting or damaging roots when putting in the stakes, position before the plant is in place.

Spring-flowering bulbs, such as daffodils and tulips, should be planted in the autumn. The tradition of lifting them every year after the foliage has died down and then storing them in a dry place until autumn involves a lot of unnecessary work and has fortunately largely died out. Now bulbs are left in the ground and require little attention other than occasionally digging them up as the foliage dies down to split them if they have become overcrowded.

Purchase new bulbs in the autumn and plant as soon as possible. The planting depth varies: for example, daffodils need to be planted about 4in (10cm) deep, tulips 6in (15cm) deep, crocuses 2in (5cm) deep and hyacinths 6in (15cm) deep. Plant where there is no need to disturb them, possibly towards the back of a border where they will show up in spring before the herbage becomes too high and where the other plants will grow quickly to cover the dying leaves.

Lifting Plants

While some bulbs are planted in the autumn, other bulbs and some of the more tender herbaceous plants such as dahlias and chrysanthemums should be lifted. Although rather exotic looking, dahlias have been grown in cottage gardens for over a century. Lift the tubers after the first frost. Then clean them of dirt and store in boxes of peat in a frost-free shed or cellar. Plant them out again once the spring frosts are past. You can also bring them into growth earlier indoors and take cuttings from the new shoots in order to start off new plants. A similar process is undertaken with chrysanthemum roots, which you should lift at the same time. Stimulate new growth towards the end of winter by bringing them into a warm greenhouse and watering and, again, taking cuttings. It is not worth replanting the old stools; plant the newly rooted cuttings.

Pruning

From late autumn through winter prune your fruit trees and shrubs. Prune apple and pear trees any time while they are out of leaf. If possible, prune plum and cherry trees only in spring, when the wounds will heal quickly thereby preventing attack by silver leaf fungus.

The purpose of pruning is to remove dead growth, to keep the tree or bush open to light and air, to maintain a pleasing shape and to help achieve the maximum quality and quantity of fruit.

Larger limbs should be cut off flush to the trunk. Smaller branches should be cut off at a 45-degree angle just above a developing bud. First any dead, dying or damaged wood should be removed. Next any branches that cross over or rub against their neighbours should be cut away. Further pruning depends on whether the fruit is carried on the tips of the shoots or on the spurs. For the former, if the branches need thinning, only the lateral shoots should be cut out. For the latter the tips of the laterals should be cut back to within three or four buds from the base to encourage the formation of fruiting spurs.

For blackcurrants and gooseberries remove all weak growth and a third of the oldest stems. For red- and whitecurrants, after taking out any dead or weak growth, shorten all laterals that arise from

LIFTING TENDER HERBACEOUS PLANTS
Some herbaceous plants are too tender to stay outside during the winter. If you want to save them for another year, lift them carefully after the first frost. Brush the loose dirt from them.

In a clean box filled with peat, cover the tubers and gently tamp down the peat. Store the box in a frost-free shed or cellar. Leave them there until all danger of frost is past and they can be planted outside.

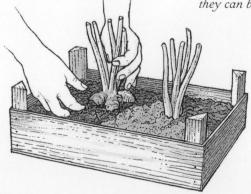

PRUNING *If you are removing a large branch, you will need to do it in stages. To prevent the branch splitting, first make a partial cut underneath the* branch about 10in (25cm) from the main stem. Then make a second cut from above, 1in (2.5cm) closer in to the tree trunk.

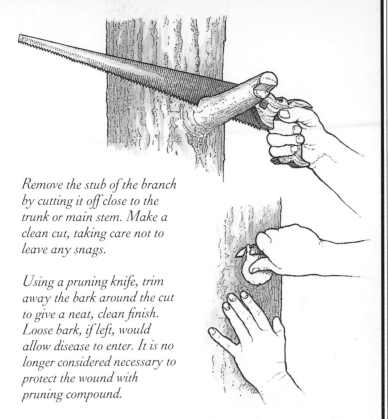

Remove the stub of the branch by cutting it off close to the trunk or main stem. Make a clean cut, taking care not to leave any snags.

Using a pruning knife, trim away the bark around the cut to give a neat, clean finish. Loose bark, if left, would allow disease to enter. It is no longer considered necessary to protect the wound with pruning compound.

the main stems to two or three buds and cut back leaders by about a third of their length to an outward-facing bud. With summer fruit, such as raspberries, cut out all the old wood and tie the new growth to the wires in its place.

For climbers, such as roses, cut out all dead wood and thin by removing some of the oldest wood if necessary. Not a great number of ornamental shrubs were grown in cottage gardens but if you have vigorous shrubs that bear flowers in early summer on new growth, prune soon after flowering. If you prune this type of shrub too late, you will remove the buds for the following season. Remove dead and over-crowded growth as well as cutting out the old flowering stems to promote new growth. Similar shrubs that flower after midsummer should be pruned in the winter in the same way.

Clearing Up

Autumn is the time for clearing up and preparing for the following year. Cut off old foliage and flowering stems and either compost or burn. Rake up leaves and stack for use when they have rotted down. All this happens in an ideal world. In the real one all this usually gets left until the spring when these jobs have to be added to the other tasks awaiting attention at that time of year. There are advantages to leaving the

clearing up of the previous season's growth. To a certain extent the dead foliage and stems protect the crown of the plant from the frosts. Any seed heads provide food for birds. The disadvantages are that in a mild winter the slugs and snails seem to hide under every leaf lying around and, of course, to the tidy-minded the garden can look terribly scruffy. The rush in spring tips the balance and it is usually best to clear up as much as possible in the autumn.

It is a good thing, particularly if your soil is heavy, to start the winter digging as soon as possible. This leaves the soil open for the action of the weather to break it down, and for the birds to get at the insect pests. There is no doubt that it makes a lot of difference to the spring workload if you can start in the autumn. Digging can continue into the winter so long as it is not too wet.

Many leaves are burnt in the autumn. This is a tremendous waste of resources, as leaf-mould is one of the most precious commodities in the garden. Leaves should be stacked, in a wire netting cage to prevent them from blowing around, until they have rotted down to a rich, crumbly consistency. This is then a useful addition to potting compost or, if you have enough of it, as a mulch on the flower borders. Leaf-mould holds moisture in dry spells, is rich in nutrients and helps break down the soil.

USING THE PRODUCE

COUNTRY PEOPLE HAVE ALWAYS BEEN used to providing for their immediate needs. There was rarely a shop just around the corner and it was often a long trudge to market. The little money that they had would have been spent on essentials that the cottager could not grow or make himself.

Drink was nearly always made in the home: cider and beer were the main beverages, and wine, which often needed expensive sugar, was used for more special occasions. Many of these drinks would have been rough to our palates, but their modern counterparts are excellent and far better than the mass-produced equivalents normally offered for sale.

It was necessary to preserve excess vegetables and fruit from the summer to supplement the food of the darker months of winter: bottling, pickling and making jam and chutneys were some of the commonest ways of doing so. These preserved foods would also enliven the diet, which could get monotonous at that time of year.

Cottagers learnt their skills by word of mouth and from practical experience, very rarely from books. This meant that there were very many different ways of preparing food and drink, of which the following recipes can give only an idea. Many variations can be made, depending on the ingredients available and the mood of the cook. Cooking was never a precise art and measurements were, and often still are, by the handful rather than by careful weighing out to the nearest ounce or gram. Again, this gives the cook much scope for variation in the recipes below, according to personal taste.

Drinks

Many cottagers used to make, and still do make, their own alcoholic drinks. Cider and beer would have been everyday drinks, and wine an occasional one, both in the home and in the fields while at work. Many of the modern versions seem like nectar compared to the mass-produced product usually drunk.

CIDER

Cider is one of the easiest of drinks to prepare as long as you have the means of extracting the juice from the apples. Any apples will do, although some advocate a mixture of sweet eating apples and sour cooking apples. In our village, Bramley cooking apples by themselves are found to be more than adequate, producing an excellent cider.

The apples are crushed and then put into a cider press where the juice is squeezed from them. Traditionally,

many farms and villages owned grinders and cider presses. If you have no access to one, then you will have to apply a little ingenuity to get the juice from the apples (a modern juice extractor perhaps). The juice is then put into a barrel, preferably wooden but plastic will do. For very dry and rough ciders, this juice is left until it has finished its fermentation, the natural sugars and yeasts in the apple being sufficient to feed this process.

For a sweeter and smoother drink simply add sugar. For a medium sweetness this should be at a rate of about 1½lb (675g) sugar per gallon (4.5l) of apple juice.

The cider is ready to drink in about six months, when the fermentation has eventually ceased.

PERRY

Perry is prepared in exactly the same way as cider, except that pears are used instead of apples.

BEER

Making beer is a much more complicated business, particularly if you want to carry out all the processes commencing with malting the barley. The main problem nowadays is that few of us have a copper or other pan in which to boil large quantities of liquid. The easiest way to make beer these days is to buy brewer's malt extract.

Traditional beer

*This is a basic recipe, which makes
a very pleasant beer with
the minimum of fuss.*
2oz (56g) dried hops
1 gal (4.5l) boiling water
1lb (450g) malt extract
¹/2lb (225g) sugar
yeast

Add the hops to the water and boil for
an hour. Strain and add the malt
extract and sugar. When dissolved
and cooled to 70°F (21°C) add the
yeast. Closely cover and leave to
ferment for a week. Remove the scum
and siphon into a cask or bottles. If
you want a gaseous beer use bottles
and add a pinch of sugar to each
before securing with a screw top.

WINE

Country people have made wine for
countless generations. Basically, it is
the juice of a fruit bulked up with
water and then fermented with the aid
of yeast and sugar.

It should be easy to make, and it is
if several simple precautions are
taken. The main one is that all vessels
and containers are scrupulously
cleaned and sterilized, with special
tablets if necessary. Secondly, it is
essential to allow the carbon dioxide
produced during fermentation out,
and equally important to prevent the
vinegar fly from getting in. You can
do this by fitting an inexpensive air
lock on to the jar or barrel.

Traditionally people would have
made large barrels of wine but nowadays it is more convenient to make
smaller quantities in glass jars.

With wine-making becoming popular, you can now buy special wine
yeasts, but yeast purchased from the
baker will suffice. Use about 1 teaspoon, just enough to start the process.

Virtually anything can be used to
flavour wine, but country people
tended to make just a few varieties
from fruit or vegetables that were
readily available. Here are just a few
for you to try.

Elderberry wine

*This is a distinctively flavoured, traditional
red wine, made from the abundant
fruit of the elder bush.*
4lb (1.8kg) elderberries
1gal (4.5l) boiling water
3lb (1.4kg) sugar
yeast

Strip the berries from their stalks and
crush them in a bucket. Pour on the
boiling water and add the sugar, let it
cool to about 70°F (21°C) and then
add the yeast. Cover and leave for
three days. Strain into a barrel or dark
jar, fitting an air lock when the
fermentation has subsided a little.
Leave until the fermentation ceases,
then decant the clear liquid.

Elderberry wine can be very strong in
its own right, but country people
sometimes make it even stronger by
adding a wine glass of brandy to each
gallon of wine.

Other berries, such as blackberries
(which produce a rich, dark wine), can
be used to make wine in the same
way as elderberry wine.

Elderflower wine

*Elderflowers are so full of flavour that only
a few are needed to make this wine.*
1pt (570ml) elderflowers
1 gal (4.5l) boiling water
3¹/2lb (1.6kg) sugar
2 tbsp white wine vinegar or dry cider
juice of 2 lemons
¹/2lb (225g) chopped raisins (optional)
yeast

Place the measured elderflowers in a
large bowl or pot and pour the boiling
water over. Add the sugar, white
wine vinegar and the juice from the
lemons. If you like, add the chopped
raisins. Allow the liquid to cool to
about 70°F (21°C) and then add the
yeast. Closely cover and leave the
liquid to ferment in a warm place for
about five days. Strain and place in a
jar with an air lock. When the liquid
has stopped fermenting and is clear it
can be decanted and bottled.

Parsnip wine

*Another traditional wine, this time made
from vegetables grown in the garden.*
4lb (1.8kg) parsnips
1gal (4.5l) water
juice of 2 lemons
3lb (1.4kg) sugar
yeast

Cut up the parsnips and then gently
boil them in the water and the juice of
the lemons until they are just soft. Do
not let them disintegrate or go
mushy. Strain the liquor and add the
sugar to it. When cooled to 70°F
(21°C) add yeast and cover. Allow to
ferment in a warm room for five days
and then place in glass jars with an air
lock. When fermentation ceases, decant into bottles.

Dandelion wine

While not deliberately grown in the garden, dandelions were found in abundance in the hedgerows and fields during the spring.
6pt (3.4l) dandelion heads
1 gal (45l) boiling water
1 lemon
1 orange
3lb (1.4kg) sugar
yeast

Place the dandelion heads in a large bowl. Add the boiling water to the flowers and leave, covered, for two days, stirring occasionally. Strain off the liquor and boil for fifteen minutes along with the shredded lemon and orange peel (no pith). Strain and add the sugar. Allow to cool to 70°F (21°C) and add the yeast. Closely cover and allow to ferment for four days. Put in a jar with an air lock and leave in a warm room until fermentation ceases, then bottle.

Rhubarb wine

This is another widely produced, traditional wine.
5lb (2.3kg) red rhubarb
1gal (4.5l) boiling water
juice of 1 lemon
3lb (1.4kg) sugar
yeast

Wipe the rhubarb clean and then chop and crush it. Add the water and leave, closely covered, for three days. Stir occasionally. Pour off the liquor and add the lemon juice, sugar and yeast. Put into a jar and fit an air lock. Bottle when fermentation ceases.

MEAD

This is one of the oldest alcoholic drinks made by the cottager.

Traditional mead

Pale honey produces a delicate, dry flavour; dark honey is best used with spices to make a strong, sweet mead.
4lb (1.8kg) honey
1gal (4.5l) water
juice of 2 lemons
pinch of tannin (or 2 cooking apples)
yeast

In a saucepan place the honey and the water and heat until the honey dissolves. Add the juice of the lemons, tannin and yeast and put into a jar with a fermentation lock. Leave until fermentation ceases, which can take a year with mead, and then bottle.

Sometimes spices, such as cinnamon, ginger and cloves, are added to the water in the initial stages to make a spicier drink.

SLOE GIN

This is a drink always associated with the country. The sloes are found growing on blackthorn bushes, which were used to form hedgerows.

Country sloe gin

Sloes turn gin a rich, ruby-red colour. This drink is wonderful when used as an after-dinner liqueur.
sloes
castor sugar
almond essence
dry gin

Half fill a kilner or similar jar with sloes that have been pricked with a fork or needle. To this add 3 to 4oz (84 to 112g) sugar, a few drops of

almond essence, and pour in the gin until the jar is full. Seal the jar and shake regularly over the next couple of months. Decant the gin, straining it several times through a folded muslin cloth if you want a clear drink.

HERB TEAS & TISANES

Cottagers were not only renowned for their alcoholic drinks. Many refreshing herbal teas and tisanes were also widely brewed in the countryside. These were achieved simply by pouring boiling water on to the leaves and flowers, fresh or dried, of certain plants and leaving them to infuse for a few minutes before straining and drinking. An ordinary teapot should not be used as it will taint the herb tea strongly. Herb teas taste best without milk; sugar or honey can be taken if you like.

Herbs suitable for infusing and drinking by themselves or in combinations are angelica, bergamot, chamomile, lemon balm, marjoram, peppermint, sage and thyme. Petals from flowers such as elderflower, hibiscus, hyssop, jasmine, lavender or roses can also be used for herb teas.

Preserves

Country people have always stored away food during times of plenty for the months when it is short. There are many ways of preserving food, but those that have come down to us are mainly the more appealing methods, such as producing jams and chutneys. A row of jars containing bottled fruit, jam and pickles also has visual appeal.

JAMS

Jam-making is still widely practised today in both country and town. It is very difficult to find a mass-produced jam that can compare with the home-made variety.

The skill in making jam is to get it to set. Some fruit, such as currants, plums and gooseberries, set more readily than others, strawberries being one of the most difficult. In the past, the easiest way was to go on boiling until the sugar formed a saturated solution that thickened the jam. Unfortunately this continuous boiling considerably reduced the flavour and spoilt the colour of the jam. The modern methods involve catching the right moment when jam will naturally set, which is approximately ten to fifteen minutes after the jam begins to boil, when the temperature reaches 220°F (105°C).

You will need a large saucepan or, preferably, a preserving pan, and a jam thermometer at hand.

Use good quality, firm fruit, on the under-ripe side (never over-ripe). Carefully wipe the fruit clean and put in the preserving pan, crushing one or two. Soften either by gently heating or, with harder fruit such as black-currants, stewing in a little water until quite tender. Add sugar and heat gently until it is all dissolved. Increase the temperature and bring to the boil. Boil vigorously and, after about ten minutes, test to see whether the jam will set. Do this by removing the pan from the heat and dropping a small amount on to a saucer and letting it cool. If the jam is ready to set, it will wrinkle when pushed with the finger. If not, it should be put back on the heat and tried again in a few minutes. An alternative is to use a jam thermo-meter, which will indicate when the jam is near setting at 220°F (105°C). Confirm this with the finger test explained above.

When the jam is ready, pour it immediately into sterilized, warm jam jars, which should be standing on several layers of newspaper in case of spillage. Lids should be applied straight away or left until the jam is completely cold. Wipe clean with a warm cloth. Label and store in a cool, dark cupboard.

Strawberry jam
Small, firm strawberries produce by far the best flavour.
4lb (1.8kg) strawberries
3¹/₂lb (1.6kg) sugar
juice of 1 lemon

Plum jam
Removing the stones from the plums can be time-consuming but it is well worth the effort for such a tasty jam.
4lb (1.8kg) plums
4lb (1.8kg) sugar
³/₄pt (430ml) water

Raspberry jam
Although raspberry jam is considered rather full of pips by some people, it does have a wonderfully subtle flavour.
4lb (1.8kg) raspberries
4lb (1.8kg) sugar

Rhubarb jam
Instead of ginger, try adding the zest of an orange or two.
4lb (1.8kg) rhubarb
4lb (1.8kg) sugar
juice and rinds of 2 lemons
1¹/₂oz (42g) bruised root ginger
(keep the ginger and lemon rinds in a muslin bag and remove before bottling)

Blackberry jam
For the best results blackberries should be harvested on a warm, dry day in early autumn.
4lb (1.8kg) blackberries
4lb (1.8kg) sugar
juice of 1 lemon

Marrow jam
Marrows are used mainly to add bulk and texture to this jam, which actually has a fresh, gingery taste.
4lb (1.8kg) prepared marrow
4lb (1.8kg) sugar
4oz (112g) crystallized ginger
juice of 2 lemons

PICKLING

Another way of preserving vegetables through the winter was to pickle them in vinegar. The prime candidates for the process were small onions, small cucumbers (or gherkins) and, of course, eggs, which were often in short supply during the period when the chickens were moulting.

A pickling vinegar can be purchased or ordinary malt vinegar can be used. If you like, add spices such as cloves, mace, allspice, cinnamon, peppers and bay leaves. You can steep them in vinegar for several weeks before straining and using or storing.

Pickled onions

Skin small pickling onions or shallots and put in brine for 24 hours. Rinse and dry. Pack into jars and pour vinegar in until the jar is nearly full. Seal and leave the onions several months before using.

Pickled gherkins

Soak the gherkins or young cucumbers in brine for a couple of days and then repeat. Dry and pack into jars and cover with vinegar.

Pickled beetroot

Use young, tender beetroot. Clean without breaking the skins and simmer in water for 1½ hours. When cold, skin and cut into slices. Pack into jars and cover with vinegar.

Pickled walnuts

Pick young, green walnuts, whose shells have not formed. Prick with a fork or needle and steep in brine for a fortnight, changing the brine after the first week. Drain and leave in the sun, turning occasionally, until they turn black. Pack into jars and add enough vinegar to cover them.

Pickled eggs

Pack shelled, hard-boiled eggs into a jar and pour vinegar over them and seal. Leave for a few weeks.

CHUTNEYS

Chutneys were a good way of using up fruit and vegetables, at the same time producing a flavoursome addition to brighten the monotony of the winter diet. They can be made of virtually any combination. Below are some of the more popular recipes to which many variations can be made.

Some of the vegetables, particularly marrows, must have water removed from them by covering them with salt for 24 hours and then rinsing and thoroughly drying. Simmer the ingredients until all the vegetables and fruit are reduced to a soft pulp and the liquid reduced so that it is not too runny. Bottle while still hot and cover with airtight lids.

Apple chutney

This chutney is perfect with pork.
3lb (1.4kg) cooking apples, peeled, cored, and chopped
1lb (450g) onions, chopped
1½lb (675g) soft brown sugar
½lb (225g) sultanas
1 teaspoon salt
2pt (1.1l) malt vinegar

Marrow chutney

This mild chutney is good with cold meats.
4lb (1.8kg) prepared marrows, chopped
½lb (225g) onions, chopped
1½lb (675g) soft brown sugar
1oz (28g) ground ginger
1pt (570ml) malt vinegar

Tomato chutney

Try tomato chutney with bacon and eggs.
6lb (2.7kg) red tomatoes, chopped
2lb (900g) apples, peeled, cored, and chopped
1lb (450g) onions, chopped
10oz (280g) sultanas
1oz (28g) salt
1oz (28g) ground ginger
1 oz (28g) mustard seed
1lb (450g) soft brown sugar
¾pt (430ml) malt vinegar

Green tomato chutney

Serve this chutney with cheese meals.
4lb (1.8kg) green tomatoes, chopped
1lb (450g) onions, chopped
1lb (450g) cooking apples, peeled, cored and chopped
½oz (14g) root ginger, minced
¼ tsp cayenne pepper
½oz (14g) salt
½lb (225g) soft brown sugar
½pt (280ml) white vinegar

Plum chutney

Plum chutney is excellent with lamb.
3lb (1.4kg) plums, stoned and chopped
1lb (450g) onions, chopped
2lb (900g) cooking apples, peeled, cored, and chopped
1oz (28g) salt
1oz (28g) allspice
1oz (28g) peppercorns
1lb (450g) soft brown sugar
1pt (570ml) malt vinegar

BOTTLING

Bottling is nowhere near as common as it once was. In a way it is the equivalent to tinned fruit except that the housewife could produce her own, using fruit from the garden or hedgerow. The deep freeze has now superseded it in most households, but

there are some fruit, such as pears, which do not freeze very well and are better bottled. Another advantage of bottled fruit is that it is instantly available. It is a suitable method of preserving most fruit, including cherries, plums, currants, raspberries, strawberries, gooseberries, blackberries, apples and pears.

The aim is to kill off all the germs in the fruit or the surrounding liquid, which will produce moulds or fermentation, and then maintain these sterile conditions until the fruit is eaten. The boiling action takes away some of the flavour and colour of the fruit, but they are still most welcome in winter, especially as fruit is scarce at that time of the year. They can be used in puddings or tarts or just served by themselves as stewed fruit, with cream or custard.

Special glass jars such as Kilner jars are used that have a screw or spring top which seals them. Rubber rings are used as a seal between the jar and the glass lid. Make certain that the rubber is in perfect condition and that it has not perished.

Only perfect, firm fruit should be used. After cleaning, firmly pack it into the jars, using, if necessary, a wooden spoon to push gently into place. Peel, core and section pears and apples before packing. Then top up the jars with cold water or syrup (½lb/225g sugar dissolved in 1pt/670ml water). Place the rubber seals and glass lids in position and screw down the metal bands.

Place the filled jars in a large pan of cold water that contains a false bottom or slats of wood, as the jars must not touch the bottom of the pan while being heated. Cover the jars with water, then slowly heat and keep simmering at 160°F (72°C) for ten minutes for most of the soft fruit, and at 180°F (82°C) for fifteen minutes for apples, pears, plums and rhubarb.

Remove the jars from the pan with an oven glove and stand on a wooden board and firmly screw down the caps before the jars cool.

SALTING

This method of preserving was widely used for runner and French beans. Whether the cost of the salt would justify it nowadays, with beans being so cheaply available from shops, is somewhat debatable.

Prepare the beans in the normal way by top-and-tailing, stringing and slicing them. Place in a large jar in alternate layers with the salt (crushed block salt) using 1lb salt (450g) per 3lb (1.4kg) beans, starting and finishing the jar with a layer of salt.

Seal. Top up after a few days when the beans have shrunk. Tightly seal the jar and store it in a cool place.

To use the beans, rinse in warm water and then soak in cold water for two to three hours. Cook as normal in fresh water.

DRYING

Drying was a common method of preserving fungi and fruit. It is still useful for storing mushrooms for an extended period, as they are not satisfactory subjects for freezing as they go slimy when defrosted.

Remove the stems from fresh-picked mushrooms and place them on paper in a moderate oven until they are thoroughly dried. Alternatively, you can thread them on pieces of string and hang them over a range or stove. They are stored by hanging, or putting in paper bags, in a cool, airy place until needed.

Herbs should be picked while young and before they flower, and hung near a stove until dry. If hung in a paper bag while drying, they are kept clean, but are not so attractive.

Certain fruit can also be dried. Apples can be cored, cut into rings and dried – traditionally threaded on sticks – in an oven until no juice can be squeezed out of them. Similarly, dark plums can be stoned and baked in an oven until dry.

INDEX

Page numbers in *italic* refer to the illustrations

ACKNOWLEDGMENTS

Authors' Acknowledgments

THE AUTHORS would like to thank Francis and David Hibbert at Axeltree Nursery and Elisabeth Strangman at Washfield Nursery for providing plants, and Sam Golding for help with gardening techniques.

Photographer's Acknowledgments

JACQUI HURST would like to thank everybody who allowed her to photograph their gardens for this book: Mr and Mrs Backholer, Mr and Mrs Belson, Mr and Mrs Boore, Mrs Boundy, Jenny and Peter Bousefield, Allan Bremner, Audrey Brickell, Richard Britain, Mr and Mrs Budge, Mr and Mrs Case, John Codrington, Ian Cole, Peggy Cole, Mrs Cowdale, Mrs Cox, Mr and Mrs Craighead, Mrs Dallmeyer, Alison and Steve Dane, Liz and James Dodds, Kim and Bill Donaldson, Susan Farquhar, Claudia and Pete Ferguson-Smyth, Mr and Mrs Fuller, Mr and Mrs Goodman, Dorothy Gorst, Bernard and Grace Hedleigh, Mrs Harding-Roberts, Janet Henderson, Mrs Holland, Mrs Hopper, Hannah Hutchinson, John and Oriel Jones, Mr Jones, Mr and Mrs Judgson, Prof Humphrey and Avril Kay, Joy Larkcom, Frank and Margery Lawley, Joan Lauè, Sophie Leaning, Lisa List, Mr and Mrs Lloyd, Mrs Malins, Henry McDonald, Mr and Mrs G H McKnight, Mary McMurtrie, Mr and Mrs Miller, Henry Moore, Major and Mrs Mordaunt-Hare, Frances Mount, Andrew and Dodo Norton, Oliver's Orchard, Mrs Payne, Mrs Pedder, Margaret and Derek Phillips, Mr and Mrs Polanska, Don Pollark, Kim and Penny Pollit, Cecilia and Tommy Price, Mrs Pritchard, Chris and Mike Ratnett, Faith Raven, Jo Rhymers, Kate Riddleston, Col and Mrs George Rouse, Willie Sandison, Mark and Alison Scott, Joan and Brian Shackleton, Mrs Shuker, Thomas Sinclaire, Jenny Spiller, David Stuart, James Sutherland, Mrs Thomson, Mr and Mrs Upton, Rosemary Verey, Sarah Waddams, Zillah and Charles Wallace, Colin Ward, Mr and Mrs Williams and Mr and Mrs Wilson. I would also like to thank Louise Arnould and David Robertson for their invaluable support.

Publisher's Acknowledgments

DORLING KINDERSLEY would like to thank the National Trust, and Thompson & Morgan for supplying seed catalogues; Hilary Bird for the index; Jane Aspden, Liza Bruml, Jo Weeks, Kate Grant, Mary-Clare Jerram and Sean Moore for editorial help; Michel Blake, Maryann Rogers and Fenella Smart for help with production.

Full-colour illustrations by Eric Thomas.
Line illustrations by Vana Haggerty, Donald Myall, Richard Phipps and Rodney Shackell.

Picture Credits

All photographs by Jacqui Hurst except where otherwise stated.
6 Cecil Tonsley (editor), *British Bee Journal*; *9* Mary Evans Picture Library; *10* Institute of Agricultural History and Museum of English Rural Life, University of Reading; *13* Mary Evans Picture Library; *14* Institute of Agricultural History and Museum of English Rural Life, University of Reading; *21* Boys Syndication; and *22, 32, 42, 53, 57, 60* and *75* Dorling Kindersley Picture Library.

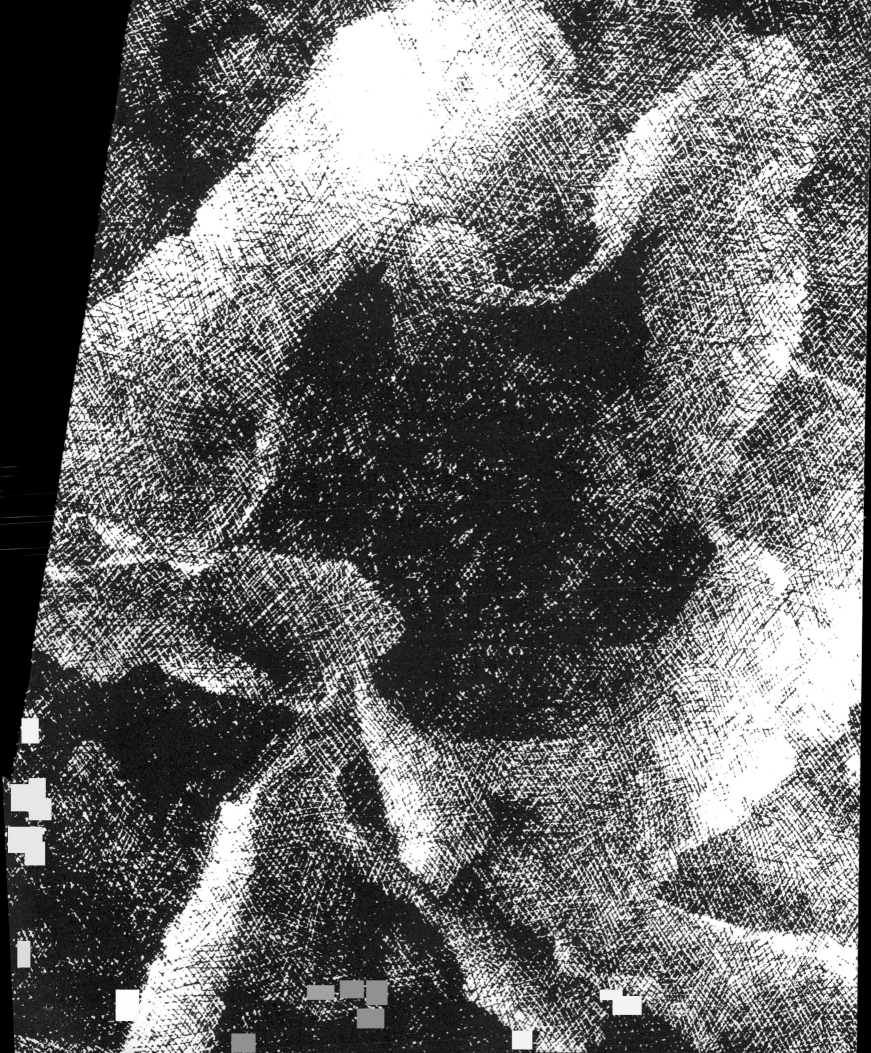